NAIL THE RECRUITING PROCESS

The Data Driven GEAR You Need to Become a College Athlete

JARED ZEIDMAN

NAIL THE RECRUITING PROCESS
© Copyright 2024 Jared Zeidman. All rights reserved.

No part of this publication may be reproduced, distributed, or transmitted in any form or by any means, including photocopying, recording, or other electronic or mechanical methods, without the prior written permission of Jared Zeidman or JZC3 LLC, except in the case of brief quotations embodied in critical reviews and certain other noncommercial uses permitted by copyright law.

Although the author and publisher have made every effort to ensure that the information in this book was correct at press time, the author and publisher do not assume and hereby disclaim any liability to any party for any loss, damage, or disruption caused by errors or omissions, whether such errors or omissions result from negligence, accident, or any other cause.

Adherence to all applicable laws and regulations, including international, federal, state, and local governing professional licensing, business practices, advertising, and all other aspects of doing business in the US, Canada, or any other jurisdiction is the sole responsibility of the reader and consumer.

Neither the author nor the publisher assumes any responsibility or liability whatsoever on behalf of the consumer or reader of this material. Any perceived slight of any individual or organization is purely unintentional.

The resources in this book are provided for informational purposes only and should not be used to replace the specialized training and professional judgment of a health care or mental health care professional.

Neither the author nor the publisher can be held responsible for the use of the information provided within this book. Please always consult a trained professional before making any decision regarding treatment of yourself or others.

For more information, email RecruitingGEAR@gmail.com

ISBN: 979-8-9896066-0-3

Cover and Interior Design by FormattedBooks

WORK WITH ME FOR FREE

Do you want to receive free guidance on the college recruiting process? If so, you can be a part of my podcast. You and your guidance will be made available for other recruits and families to learn from you, but your session with me will be free! For more information, visit https://NailTheRecruitingProcess.com

ACKNOWLEDGEMENTS

This project wouldn't have gotten done without some key players, and I'd like to dedicate this to them.

My Family

Thank you for continuing to support me and show me light when I most needed it over these past two years. I'll never forget the ways in which you lifted me and directed me when I needed it most. Thank you for believing I could be anything if I bet on myself and was resilient. Even if none of us thought that would ultimately result in me becoming an author, here we are! Mom, Dad, Jesse, and Jamie, thank you for everything. I love you.

My People

I'm blessed to have the best friends and mentors in the universe. You know who you are, and you know what you've done for me. To my Port people, my QU people, my Buffalo people (parts 1 and 2), and my Capital Region people: Thank you for supporting the person I am while also challenging me to continue growing. Thank you for your patience with me when I was... you know... a handful. I love you all.

My Boo

I am better at everything because of you. I am a better person, coach, friend, listener, and partner. I know you want me to say that I also now have a better fashion sense because of you, but I just can't give you that one. I hope you can settle for knowing that you make me better in every other way. There is no one in this world who inspires me more than you. Thank you for having my back when I wasn't even sure I had my own. I love you more than anything in this world. Don't tell Lola.

HEY YOU!

Yes, you! I just wanted to quickly remind you that no matter what happens in your recruiting process, there is so much more to you than your sport. The things that make you a great teammate, friend, family member, and person are all more important than your sport. Being an athlete is one of the many things you do, but it is not who you are. In your moments of doubt during the recruiting process, remember this:

YOU ARE MORE THAN THE SPORT YOU PLAY.

CONTENTS

Introduction xi

SECTION 1
BUILDING A SOLID FOUNDATION

1. Myth Busting: How College Coaches Actually Think.... 3
2. Get in Gear. 21
3. What's Most Important? 31

SECTION 2
GROW

4. Finding Your Mentors 47
5. Growing Your Network 57
6. Growing Your Game 75

SECTION 3
FINDING YOUR FIT

7. Unofficial Campus Visits 89
8. Official Campus Visits 107
9. Committing and Beyond 121

CCQ Questionnaire Data 127
Anecdotal Notes 137

INTRODUCTION

So, you want to be a college athlete? First off, you have to get confirmation that you're good enough at your sport to play it at the collegiate level. Then comes finding the right school and the right team. That first step of simply finding the right school can be overwhelming for anyone. Then, if you want to be an athlete, you're signing up for double trouble by throwing choosing a team into the mix. A good friend of mine in coaching said it perfectly: "If you're looking to be a college athlete, you're likely making the two toughest choices you've made in your life, at the same time."

The process of making these choices is complex, which is why it's easy to make mistakes. Especially if you're the first prospective college student *and* college athlete in your family. That means double jeopardy - you may not understand the process of getting recruited or the process of applying to a college. This can lead to a series of avoidable mistakes. College coaches that see someone in your position make one of those mistakes tend to turn to their colleagues and say something along the lines of, "that kid got bad advice." I'm here to give you good advice.

JARED ZEIDMAN

Who am I? My name is Jared, and I'm going to help you nail the recruiting process. Even after nearly 15 years spent around college basketball, I'm still fascinated by the recruiting process. It allows me to imagine what a team could look like in the future by mapping it out like a puzzle, with recruiting serving as the way to find the right pieces. Over the years I've gotten pretty good at it, found great satisfaction in it, and gained the respect of my peers.

It all led to me working a dream job, as an assistant coach at Canisius University (a Division I program) in Buffalo, New York. Then that dream was shattered. In April of 2022, I got COVID-19 for the first time, and almost immediately experienced issues with my immune system that would keep me from coaching indefinitely.

My recovery process reminded me of all the courageous athletes I worked with as they navigated injury rehab, grief, illness, and doubt. Even if I couldn't coach, I knew I wanted to keep working with courageous young people, so I began working with some high school-aged students who aspired to play basketball in college. Certain pain points began cropping up consistently in my early conversations with them, and in general it seemed like neither they nor their families really knew how to make sense of interactions with college coaches.

So, I did what I've always done - I came up with a game plan. I wanted to write a manuscript that would help high school athletes and their families nail the college recruiting process. It would address every part of the journey, and be informed by the input of the college coaching community. Please note, I didn't just say "college *basketball* coaching community."

NAIL THE RECRUITING PROCESS

While this project started out as basketball oriented, the responses from basketball coaches were so consistent that I started to wonder if this content could be applicable to all prospective college athletes.

I ended up interviewing and surveying 50 coaches, including a contingent of fall and spring sport coaches at both the scholarship and non-scholarship levels of intercollegiate athletics. After collecting that data, I interviewed current and former college athletes to learn what they valued most in their recruiting processes, as well as what they regretted most. Many disconnects emerged in this process, and I was certain that a book about it would really help recruits and their families.

The rest of this book is designed in a way that will walk you through every phase of this process, from the VERY beginning - exploring your own values, finding the right mentors, networking with college coaches, growing as an athlete, visiting campuses, signing day, and EVERYTHING in between.

While basketball will be used to give examples and anecdotes—because it is the sport I am most familiar with—you should be able to easily apply these examples to any sport you're interested in. For the sake of brevity throughout the book, the acronym CCQ will be used, which stands for "college coaches questioned." If you see a number along with the acronym, it means that the coaches were asked to scale something between 1 and 10. A 1 means they either completely disagreed or it never happens in their program, and a 10 that they completely agreed, or it always happens in their program.

THIS SOUNDS INTERESTING... WHAT'S THE CATCH?

There is no catch. I'm a life-long dork, and actually went to college to be a journalist. Then I took some weird left turns and became a college administrator. Then I started coaching basketball. Then I got really sick. And now here I am. This project allows me to combine every skill I've developed over the course of my life to help YOU.

The part where you continue to grow as an athlete and master your sport is still up to you. But I can promise you one thing. If you and your family finish this book, you will have a leg up in this process on the recruits and families that haven't. In this book, you will learn skills that won't just help you in the recruiting process, but also for what life is actually like as a college athlete.

You ready?

Let's rock.

SECTION 1

BUILDING A SOLID FOUNDATION

MYTH BUSTING: HOW COLLEGE COACHES ACTUALLY THINK

Let's play a quick game. I'm going to give you three different people. You're going to tell me what these people have in common.

PERSON 1: A top recruit, with high talent, who we recruited heavily. They committed before their senior playing season in high school even started.

PERSON 2: A very talented recruit, local to our school, who we recruited heavily through their senior year of high school. They committed in their senior spring.

PERSON 3: A recruit with a great attitude and work ethic who we weren't sure we had a spot for, so we told them they would need to try out in the fall of their first year of college and make the team.

What do those three people have in common?

All three of them ended up having great careers, became team captains by their senior year, and were highly respected by their teammates and coaches.

Now, let's play another game. What do all three of these players have in common?

PERSON 1: A top recruit, with high talent, who we recruited heavily and got to commit before their senior playing season in high school even started.

PERSON 2: A very talented recruit local to our school, who we recruited heavily through their senior year, and committed senior spring.

PERSON 3: A recruit with a great attitude and work ethic who we weren't sure we had a spot for, so we told them that they would need to try out in the fall and make the team.

What do those three people have in common?

All three stopped playing college basketball after their first year.

Here's the biggest thing you need to know about recruiting, right off the rip:

IT'S NOT AN EXACT SCIENCE.

The glitz and glamor of televised intercollegiate athletics may lead you to believe that college coaches always nail the recruiting process, getting it right every time. Nope! In reality, that's simply not true. There are tons of variables in this process.

Some players get hurt. Some players fall out of love with the sport they chose. Some players fall more in love with other parts of college. Some players feel like they picked the right coaching staff but wrong school. Some players feel like they picked the right school but wrong coaching staff. Some kids feel like they were misled in the recruiting process, or mistreated as an athlete by their coaches, and elect to transfer or stop playing. Some coaches feel like players did not give an honest impression of themselves during the recruiting process, and make cuts.

The recruiting process can get messy. And to sift through one big mess, you need…

One Big Filter

That's how I want you to visualize your recruiting process - one big filter. You go through all of your experiences, and only the good quality experiences make it through the filter. While you sift your experiences through your filter, coaches do the same through theirs, and ultimately what comes out the end of both is a mutual fit. We will get into your filter more in a little bit. I want to focus on coaching filters first, for one important reason:

You get one shot at the filtering process, but a coach has a new filter every year, and each year their filter becomes more refined.

As college coaches get more experienced, they alter their recruiting methods based on past experiences that weren't successful. For example, let's say a coach recently took a chance on a lesser recruited player with a questionable attitude, and that risk didn't pan out. That coach will then have a stronger "attitude filter" in place moving forward. Every coach has a filter, and the best coaches will do the most filtering. This book will help you develop your filter. But that can't happen before you understand the filter of your average college coach.

Alert: There's a good chance you're wrong about what's important to college coaches.

College coaches don't think the average high school recruit understands the day-to-day life of a college athlete.

This is the most important thing you need to know. It foreshadows the rest of this book. I asked college coaches if they thought the average recruit understood what college sports actually look like day-to-day, and the CCQ response was a 3.5 out of 10. Clearly, they OVERWHELMINGLY do not think you understand what it actually takes to succeed as a college athlete.

And it's not just coaches who feel that way.

The former college athletes I spoke to unanimously agree with them.

The athletes I interviewed admitted to me that they didn't understand it back then either, even after their recruiting processes were over. Every athlete I spoke to felt wholly unprepared for the physical toll that college sports would take on their bodies, and the mental toll that poor performance would take on their esteem. And that's not even taking into account the time commitment the sport itself requires!

Coaches tend to assume that a recruit has access to some other person who adequately explains the ins and outs of college sports. Most simply don't. If you want to nail the recruiting process, you need someone like this in your corner.

Nothing can fully prepare you for the transition from high school to college athletics. BUT there are skills that you can develop to help make it as smooth as possible. If you start working on these skills now, you will stand out to coaches in the recruiting process. More on this in the next chapter.

Coaches do not value your AAU/Club or high school team the way you do.

College coaches utilize AAU basketball and/or high school basketball as an opportunity to watch you play against similarly skilled competition. The name on the front of your jersey tends to not matter as much as you think it might, and the level of team you're on (i.e. Elite, Platinum, National or whatever the cool name for the top team is nowadays) is also not important.

Occasionally, there are teams that specialize in placing players in specific types of collegiate institutions, but there is currently an over saturation of both teams and competitive tournaments. Therefore, it's way more important that a coach **a)** sees you playing against competition of sufficient caliber to accurately evaluate your skill set, and **b)** affiliates you with a coach (or mentor) that can accurately speak to your strengths and limitations.

The players I spoke to found the most important parts of AAU to be mentorship and visibility, which aligns with the perspective of college coaches. For example, if you want to be a D-I athlete, you want to be on an AAU team that's playing against D-I caliber talent during a D-I live period, since that's where D-I coaches will be. If that team is coached by someone with experience at and knowledge of the D-I level that can properly advise you, it's icing on the cake.

When it comes to the raw data, the CCQ scored the importance of being on a prestigious AAU/Club team at a 4.25 out of 10, and a prestigious high school basketball team at a 3.28. Coaches understand that most players don't have a choice in where they go to high school. In fact, a coach that recently went to a final four in their sport told me they didn't think they had a single player on their team that could afford being on the best AAU team or best private high school team in their region.

Plain and simple: A college coach's job is to find you. If you're good enough to play at the level they coach, they're going to find you 99 out of 100 times (and don't worry we will also prepare for that 1/100 time, just in case.)

I have coached several successful college athletes with limited or zero AAU/Club experience. So has every great coach I know. If you're going the club route, choose to play for the best mentor available, who will consistently get you in front of the eyes you want to ultimately play for.

The current position you play does not matter, neither do your stats.

To prove it, I asked the CCQ how often athletes recruited at a specific position actually play that position throughout their college careers. The average response was 3. The most common response was a 1. Rather than gauge a position fit, coaches tend to think more broadly and evaluate potential system fits. Most high school positions and statistics do not reflect college system fits in ANY sport.

Are there exceptions? Yes, of course. If a D-I softball coach knows they need a pitcher, they may rely on specific stats that can help them narrow down their recruiting targets. Similarly, if a D-III football team knows they need a quarterback, they may recruit with that position as their top priority. But you need to know that these exceptions end up applying to a much smaller percentage of the total recruiting body than many people think. Most athletes continue growing and developing substantially during their time in college. They change. And so do their positions.

Coaches will consult specific stats when applicable (i.e. batting average, free throw percentage, golf score etc.), but general stats do not account for the quality of your competition. Your stats will not replace the eye test, and you will still need to pass it.

College coaches do not care if you are a single sport athlete in high school. The data suggests they actually prefer otherwise.

The average CCQ response on this was 1.5. That response did not change at any competitive level, or across gender of sport. While it might sound crazy, it actually makes perfect sense.

Ever heard the word "coachable" before (i.e. "this kid is super coachable")?

Take a second here. Think critically about what that means. A coachable athlete can take feedback or constructive criticism without getting in their own head and taking the feedback personally.

How does an athlete become coachable? THEY GET COACHED OFTEN, AND BY DIFFERENT PEOPLE!

The feedback I received from both players and coaches strongly suggests that the more unique coaching experiences you have in middle and high school, the more coachable you'll go on to be in college. The more sports you play, the more access you have to different coaches. Over the course of my research, I heard both basketball coaches and former basketball players credit a non-basketball coach as the mentor who taught them the most about discipline and preparation.

Brace yourself. This is something that's going to be tough for you to read. There are people close to you that do not want you to believe that this is the truth. It's in the best interest of a personal trainer to keep you from playing a spring sport if you're a basketball player, or to keep you from playing basketball if you're a baseball player, and so on and so forth. There are also AAU basketball coaches that could really use you on their fall-ball rosters, even though it may keep you from playing soccer or tennis. What those coaches are less likely to share, is the emerging research indicating that a record number of youth athletes are undergoing orthopedic surgery for injuries sustained due to their single sport focus*.

All of those pressures exist. Thankfully, raw data now also exists. The belief that you need to be a single sport athlete is now officially a nothingburger. A college coach either doesn't care that you're a single sport athlete, or actually wants you to play additional sports for the sake of injury prevention and personal development.

In the time that I've been coaching, some of the most sought after recruits I built relationships with were all-state athletes in other sports. I realize this goes against what some high school trainers and AAU coaches say, but you need to act in your best interests, not theirs.

*For more information on this, please refer to the National Institute of Health Library of Medicine or refer to ESPN.com's news archives for a series of articles on the subject over the last decade

The more you (and not your parents) facilitate your recruiting process, the better your chances of finding the right program.

Two things happened in your generation that changed parental involvement in higher education.

1) The price of college has skyrocketed, outpacing wage inflation and making financing it harder than it has ever been in our country's history. College is CRAZY expensive right now, and unless you're offered a generous scholarship or merit package, your parents are likely helping you pay for it.

2) Every facet of your college experience is now easily communicated by the phone you are likely holding in your hand as you read this. When I went to college, my parents didn't have day-to-day access to what I was doing. My ups, downs, triumphs, hardships, and unbearable stupidity were not captured on camera (thank God). Yours are. The level of connection between students and their parents has increased exponentially.

The changing times have resulted in an increased level of both financial and emotional investment from parents. So, of course parents are going to be more involved in the recruiting process.

The CCQ responses indicated varying levels of patience with parents on the part of coaches. More than half the coaches said they would back off of a recruit whose parents were communicating more than the recruit was. But there are some very successful coaches out there who are willing to be more patient with parents who take the lead (more on this later in the book).

With this in mind, you taking the lead in your process can be a real differentiator. By taking the initiative, you can move yourself up a coach's ladder. This skill is particularly useful in the later stages of the recruiting process, when coaches will intentionally direct questions towards you, the future college athlete.

Coaches evaluate your attitude as much as your quality of your play.

Coaches are notorious for being stubborn. Our profession is made up of "my way or the highway" personality types. So, it's always a surprise when 50 coaches agree on something.

Here's that something.

The CCQ were given an open-ended opportunity to identify what they are evaluating besides athletic performance when they watch a recruit play live.

ALL 50 COACHES RESPONDED WITH A COMMENT ON ATTITUDE.

Successful coaches value culture. They want players that are going to dap up their teammates when something good happens and be the first to offer support when something bad happens. They want players who are engaged, even when they're on the bench. They want positive energy and unshakeable resilience.

We will talk a lot more about this later in the book, but for now I want to give you one more specific data point about attitude. Even at the highest scholarship level, college coaches are willing to take on a less talented player if they consistently demonstrate they will have the best attitude on the team. I have personally coached several of these players, and they are some of my favorite people on the planet. The more intentional you are as a recruit about developing a positive attitude, the more you will be rewarded by coaches in this process.

If you're tied with another prospective athlete on a coach's list, the offer will go to whoever is more engaged.

One of the practices I've utilized as a coach is an act called "following the heat." As we get closer to decision time, I become more inclined to extend offers to recruits I know are seriously interested in coming to my school and being part of my team.

We will talk later in the book about the process of having a "big board" and developing your top tier schools. For now, know this: If you have asked enough of the right questions, done enough homework, and are confident that a school is at or near the top of your list, YOU NEED TO COMMUNICATE THAT TO THE HEAD COACH. You will get ahead of other recruits in your position who have not done so.

Part of a college coach's filter is identifying who actually wants to play for them. If that's you, let them know! You may move up their list.

Engagement becomes even more important when your recruiting process enters the in-person stages. When you're on a campus visit, a coach can gauge if you're showing up authentically. They will also have a sense of your level of interest through your level of engagement. Much like in the working world, making the right first impression in-person goes a long way.

College Coaches are watching you. Like, REALLY watching you.

In marketing, a "touch point" is a phrase used to describe any opportunity a brand or company has to engage with you before

NAIL THE RECRUITING PROCESS

you make a decision to purchase their product. Think about your recruiting process as a series of touch points. A coach sees you play, you have a phone call with that coach, you visit their campus, you talk to current members of the team. Those are all touch points.

But they're not just touch points for you...

If you have an off moment during one of those touch points, you can be sure that it's going to be noticed and discussed by the coaching staff, no matter what stage of the process you are in. Perhaps you're on an overnight visit and you say or do something inappropriate—even if it's away from the coaches and just in front of current players—you can rest assured that a good coaching staff is going to find out about it.

Coaches are looking for the most poised athletes they can find. If you give them enough reasons during your touch points to not pursue you, they will back off. I've done it personally, and I was floored by how like-minded the CCQ were about this process. Here's a true story from my first ever AAU tournament.

I was young and extremely stupid, but very excited and coachable, so people kept me around. One of them was Mary Ellen Burt, the winningest coach in the history of Union College, a largely NCAA Division III program in Schenectady, New York. Two very specific things happened on my first AAU recruiting trip with Mary Ellen.

I sat down at the first game and furiously took notes on an incredible 6'3" forward that seemingly could do it all. When Mary Ellen sat down next to me, I enthusiastically shared my notes as if I were a Golden Retriever that had discovered a long-lost log. She quickly replied "Jared, that kid is going to UCONN."

The very next game, I had a slightly more refined eye for talent but the same amount of enthusiasm. I was watching a specific player who'd previously reached out to our staff and expressed an interest in our program. This was our first time seeing her play in person. In the first half, her team gave up three unanswered transition baskets (for non-basketball people, this is really bad). The third basket prompted her coach to call a timeout. On her way back to the bench, she ignored every high five attempted by her teammates. Then, while the coach addressed the team, she sat on the bench about 15 feet away from the huddle and took a few swigs of water from her water bottle. Coach Burt leaned over to me and said, "I've seen enough. Cross her off the list."

I may not have known exactly what D-III talent looked like, but on day one I learned what it doesn't look like - if you can't handle coaching in high school, you definitely can't handle it at the college level. College coaches use the recruiting process to determine whether or not you can take their coaching. You'd be wise to never forget that.

You will have to work through a sales pitch to find your fit.

The final filtering stages will feature a sales pitch that is unlike any you or your family are likely to have experienced before. You are being sold a product and being assessed for your ability to use that product at the same time. It's really weird and I don't think it exists anywhere else.

NAIL THE RECRUITING PROCESS

Over the last decade, recruiting visits have transformed into more glitzy family experiences, designed for a social media showcase… cool tours, photo opportunities, graphics, swag, hashtags, the works. This is where you have to know that glamorous photo-ops and slick locker rooms don't always lead to positive and rewarding student experiences.

Recent NCAA rule changes mean transferring athletes no longer have to sit out for a year after they enter a new school. This has prompted a STAGGERING number of departures. Last year, nearly 12% of the entire NCAA D-I population (20,911 people) entered the NCAA transfer portal. For those unfamiliar, the transfer portal is an online database where an NCAA player has to register if they want to transfer to another NCAA sponsored school.

If more than 1-in-10 athletes feel their experience didn't line up with their expectations, it means the recruiting process is clearly going wrong for many athletes and their families. It's hard to identify one specific cause, but here's my research backed hypothesis:

Both good and bad coaches know how to sell, and recruits don't know how to differentiate between the two.

We've already discussed some variables that could lead to a player quitting their sport or transferring to a new school. A component we haven't discussed yet is bad coaches. Many of the coaches interviewed for this book expressed wariness of other colleges with reputations for misleading recruits during the process. They specifically mentioned coaches less invested in the intrinsic and extrinsic development of their athletes, and more interested in the perks of a high visibility job.

There are some people in sales that value relationships, who always make sure their product is right for the specific customer in front of them (these are coaches you should be trying to find.) There are others in sales that know exactly what to say to make the sale, even if the math doesn't add up (these are the coaches you want to avoid.) There are also great people who are bad coaches. These are the people who struggle to consistently match their behaviors to their stated mission when it comes to leadership.

Good coaches understand that kids are kids, and kids don't always make the best decisions for themselves off the rip. Because of this, they've started doing something that I will call "re-recruiting." They intentionally save space on their rosters for transfer athletes who initially chose the wrong fit, and then start the recruiting process over with them after they leave their previous team. The transfer athletes I interviewed all went through this re-recruiting process, and shared two key factors that led them to transfer. First, they felt the actions of their coaches were not consistent with their words. Second, they felt their college was not a supportive environment for them when they most needed help.

Multiple transfer athletes described using their transfer processes to ask the questions they should have asked the first time around. If you are reading this book, your goal should be to avoid the re-recruiting process and get it right the first time. It's not easy, and it will take extra work on your end, but it's worth it for the sake of finding the right fit. You'll end up being happier. Even on your worst days as an athlete you will still feel cared about by the people closest to you, and you will still feel like you're in the right environment. This book is going to equip you with all the GEAR you need to get the recruiting process right the first time.

FOR PARENTS/GUARDIANS:

Please read this book along with your child. Look out for notes just like this at the end of each chapter to provide you with the best tools and strategies to get involved with your child's process.

 GET IN GEAR

Most college coaches don't just coach a sport for their love of that sport. They want to develop young people. More specifically, they want to help cultivate specific skills in young people. Some of these skills include communication, accountability, time management, and resilience. Those four examples merely scratch the surface.

What's the key difference between coaches and professors? Coaches choose their students. They use recruiting to identify who is most likely to succeed in their program. Based on my experience, conversations with players, and feedback from the CCQ, I've developed an acronym of the four most important qualities you need to focus on to nail this process.

I call it your recruiting GEAR.

College coaches will be assessing the quality of your GEAR. The better your GEAR is now, the more a college coach will believe you belong in their classroom. This book is going to challenge you to build and refine your recruiting GEAR. If you do it, you will not only be more prepared for the recruiting process, but also for college itself.

One more quick thing before we go over your GEAR piece by piece. No faking it. Coaches can spot inauthenticity, so you're going to need to be all in on your GEAR.

Special thanks in advance to Merriam-Webster for the definitions.

G = Growth-Oriented

Growth is defined as "progressive development," and oriented as "intellectually, emotionally, or functionally directed." Put them together and you get an individual who is intellectually and emotionally directed towards continued progressive development.

It sounds simple in theory, but in practice it's hard. Like the sport you play, this process is filled with ups and downs, great days and great pains. If you practice being growth-oriented, your mishaps will begin to bother you less, and you can apply your failures towards future growth. If you're wondering how this applies specifically to your recruiting process, here are a couple of examples:

1) You are able to communicate to coaches that you are still growing as an athlete and as a leader over the course of your high school career.
2) You are open to both building on your strengths and addressing your limitations.
3) You are able to sustain a positive attitude, even when things aren't going your way.

Remember, attitude trumps everything. The key to a great attitude in athletics is being growth-oriented. If you'd like to learn more specifically about growth, I would heavily recommend reading *Mindset* by Carol S. Dweck, and *Burn Your Goals* by Joshua Medcalf.

Your personal growth helps you AND your team, and growth-oriented personalities are contagious. Coaches at every competitive level want a growth-oriented leader on their team.

E = Engaged

One of the definitions for engaged is "greatly interested, a synonym for 'committed.'" There are many nuanced parts of the recruiting process, involving skills that develop over time. Being engaged is not one of them. Engagement is either on or off. Coaches can tell when even the quietest athlete is engaged through their eye contact, posture, and energy.

Here are the engagement practices you need to embody as a growth-oriented high school student:

1) You (not your parents) initiate and facilitate conversations with college coaches.
2) You take the initiative as a communicator on the court/field, soliciting feedback from your current coaches after practices and games.
3) Whether in the game or on the bench, you are LOCKED IN.

As I write this, I can sense some skepticism from the shy readers. Well, here's some interesting data for you. I asked the CCQ if a recruit could move up their list by being positive and engaged on their visit. The most common response was a 10. I then asked them if a disengaged visitor could move down their list, and the most common answer was also a 10.

Successful college athletes are held accountable for the ways they engage. Now that you know this, you should embrace discomfort in the name of growth and start engaging earlier. Use these engagements to your advantage while you're being recruited. It can be the deciding factor.

A = Aware

Aware means "having or showing realization, perception, or knowledge."

Now, recruit, heed my command:

KNOW THY SELF.

- What are you great at?
- What do you stink at?
- What makes you happy?
- What shuts you down?
- What do you want out of your college experience, as both a student and an athlete?

Those are just a few of the MANY things you should know about yourself if you want to confidently navigate this process.

Also, if your answer to any of the above questions was "I don't know," that's totally okay. Part of being growth-oriented is going through experiences to figure out what you like and don't like.

Don't just let your sport use you. Use your sport to better know yourself. Need some motivation to begin this practice? The CCQ strongly agreed that a prospect they are seriously recruiting should be able to speak to their own strengths and limitations. You can't know how to grow until you know where growth is needed. Ask yourself the tough questions.

There is another significant component to awareness - being mindful that you're constantly being evaluated in this process. Being aware means you are alert to your surroundings and the consequences (both good and bad) of your decisions. College athletics, and therefore athletes themselves, are often the most prominent public facing part of the school. If you have keen awareness, a coach will be confident that you can positively represent their program.

R = Ready

I'm actually going to give you Merriam-Webster's first two definitions of "ready," because they combine to be critically important here:

1) "prepared mentally or physically for some experience or action"
2) "prepared for immediate use."

If you are intentional in your focus on growing, engaging, and becoming more aware, you will develop the resilience to be ready for anything that can possibly come your way as a college athlete. Positions, schedules, playing rotations, relationships, classes, and emotions are just some of the elements that will be constantly in flux during college. And, honestly, that's just the beginning. Your ability to calmly navigate chaos will be a predictor of your ability to succeed as a college athlete.

Being ready does require acceptance. In truth, you have no idea when a coach will be watching or calling you. In the same way, you have no idea how your next tryout is going to go. But if you consistently feel prepared, you will consistently feel confident. That confidence translates to readiness.

The GEAR Guarantee

As much as I want to, I cannot guarantee that you will become a college athlete by reading this book. There is a skill floor in your sport that neither you or I can control, and each coach has their own preferences when it comes to sport-specific skills. But what I can guarantee is that by focusing on your GEAR, you will find this process rewarding and will learn a ton about yourself.

Here is a real way to test whether or not you're ready for this journey.

The next page is a contract with yourself. A pledge to develop your GEAR. An agreement to adopt this mindset from now on. I say that because you are 100% going to realize as you read

NAIL THE RECRUITING PROCESS

this book that it's worth maintaining this mindset for the rest of your time on this planet. Fold the page over so that any time you have a moment of doubt, you can re-read the contract to yourself and remember your "why." From this point on, we are going to approach your recruiting process with your GEAR in mind.

Be sure to have at least one other person sign as well. They will be there to support you when you need it, and challenge you when it's time to dig deeper.

When you're ready, sign the next page and read on.

JARED ZEIDMAN

Name:
Date:

This contract indicates that I, _____,
am fully committed to getting in GEAR for the recruiting process. I will seek out opportunities for continued growth. I will be fully present and engage in those opportunities to the best of my ability. Afterwards, I will solicit feedback about my experiences in service of becoming more aware. I believe that, by refining these skills, I will be ready for whatever challenges come my way in this process.

In my moments of doubt, I know that I have _____ and _____ to lean on. They will encourage me, but also be honest and provide constructive criticism when I need it. This process will not be easy, but neither is being a college athlete. The more I grow now, the more I will be rewarded for it in the recruiting process and beyond.

Signed:
Date:

Witness Signature(s):
Date:

FOR PARENTS/GUARDIANS:

This chapter was designed to lay out the specific skills your child needs to develop in order to put their best foot forward in the recruiting process. Future chapters will indicate more detailed steps you can take to best challenge and support them. For now, there is only one rule you need to follow:

Unless you believe your child is involved in a challenge that will negatively impact their mental or physical health, DO NOT RESCUE THEM FROM AN EXPERIENCE WHERE THEY ARE GOING TO FAIL.

I have found some parents really struggle to watch their child fail at something without intervening. Please understand that short term sadness from a mistake or failure does not lead to long term dissatisfaction. In fact, students who struggle the most in college are often those who were so protected from failure in high school that they cannot process the autonomy of young adulthood.

It will be tough to see your child struggle at certain things. Your job is not to rescue them from those struggles, but to be their lighthouse. Support them when they have doubts, remind them that receiving a blow to their self-esteem is a part of the human experience. Do not have the experience for them or shield them from it.

In the moment, it may not seem counterproductive, but in the long term you're just punting the football.

WHAT'S MOST IMPORTANT?

Now that you've gained more of an understanding of what coaches want in a recruit, it's time to bring the focus back to your filter. The GEAR we're focusing on here is awareness. The more honed your awareness is, the better you'll be able to identify potential fits. Your values and preferences should also dictate this process, and this chapter is devoted to helping you discover what's most important to you.

If you are exploring college choices for the first time, you might find the array of options overwhelming. Deciding what you value most will help narrow it down. Here are some important questions to ask yourself to jumpstart your thought process.

What do I want to major in?

This question goes first because it's the most important. Everyone dreams of it, but the overwhelming majority of college athletes will not go on to play their sport professionally. Therefore, it's crucial to find a college that has a major that interests you. This will immediately knock a lot of schools off your list, and that is okay. There are tons of choices out there.

Find one where you can match that major with a coaching staff who you know will support you.

"But I really don't know what I want to major in yet!"

That is totally okay. I changed majors twice in college, and then became a basketball coach... so I'm living proof that your interests may change as you explore new things!

That said, however, I would strongly suggest finding colleges that are best suited to supporting undecided students. comprehensive and liberal arts institutions are schools that mandate a core curriculum for all students, in which you'll spend your first two years taking classes across all disciplines. You can use those experiences to discover what is most interesting to you.

My alma mater is considered a comprehensive institution. While enrolled, I ended up minoring in sociology and doing an independent study on the sociology of intercollegiate athletics. For what it's worth, I did not take a sociology course until my sophomore year. You don't know what you don't know. But, in this instance, even not knowing can help inform your decision!

How do I want to be coached?

You will be spending more time with your college coaches than you can possibly imagine right now. There will be film sessions, study halls, bus trips, fundraisers, campus events, and many other things that will keep you near your coaches besides practices and games. So, it's really important that you know what type of coaching you respond to. Some players respond to energy, others respond to a calmer presence. Some players want a fiery and intense coach, and others can take that sort of coaching personally. Reflect on the coaching experiences that motivated you in the past, as well as the ones that shut you down.

A word of caution on this subject – if you just responded to yourself with something like, "I feel like I can be coached by anyone," you're not digging deep enough. Recruits often say similar things to coaches during the recruiting process to try and score brownie points by seeming flexible. It rarely ends up being true. A huge component to your ultimate satisfaction on a team will be playing for a coach that "gets you." Do not cheat yourself by trying to be accommodating.

Which competitive level is right for me?

Regardless of what competitive division interests you, you should be prepared for the arduous extent of the prep, participation, and body maintenance required to be a college athlete. It will take an absolute minimum of 20 hours a week when you are in-season. And it only goes up from there, depending on the level of competition.

Many youngsters set a goal of being Division I scholarship athletes because they exclusively associate D-I sports with college sports. Major NCAA D-I athletics are played in front of large live crowds and broadcasted to even larger television and streaming audiences. So that association makes sense, but in reality, it is far from the only option.

There are phenomenal coaches who have devoted their careers to developing young people at every competitive level out there. Some coaches align better with the D-III philosophy of sports being part of the greater educational mission of the school. Others love the D-I experience that allows them to focus more exclusively on the recruiting and development of their program and their athletes. Having worked at both ends of the spectrum, I can tell you that both have their pros and cons.

If you are a non-scholarship athlete, you will still be substantially committed to your sport, but that will lessen when you are not in your playing season. It's therefore more common for those in non-scholarship levels to be multi-sport athletes, and athletes who are more involved in campus communities outside of their sport.

In the time I coached at the D-III level, during the preseason, my team practiced five times a week and also worked out with a strength and conditioning coach three times a week. During the playing season, one or two of those practices per week were replaced by games, but practices tended to be longer because there would be scouting film to prepare for upcoming games. The best players would also watch extra film at least once a week, and do extra on-court work with myself or another coach. Once the season ended, players had one performance meeting with a coach. After that, aside from seeing students at campus events and academic check-ins, our interactions were pretty limited. The athletes still lifted as a team 3-4 times a week and played pick-up basketball on their own, but they weren't coached.

There were some athletes at the D-III level that wanted to be doing way more than they were, and there were also those who were not expecting the commitment at the D-III level to be as intense as it was. That said, the best D-III athletes I saw there were those that chose D-III for more balance in their student lives, but were still fully committed as athletes.

The scholarship level is everything I just mentioned, but more intense. More pre-and-post season workouts, events and engagements, and significantly more time spent with teammates and coaches. At the highest levels of scholarship athletics, it is run like a business. That means you need to mean business, particularly when it comes to putting in the amount of time you're expected to. In exchange for this investment, there are a lot of unique perks in addition to a partial or full scholarship. Awesome equipment and swag, travel opportunities, NIL related endorsements, upgraded facilities, access to more support staff, and the opportunity to compete at the highest level are just some of what come to mind.

In my experience working with and talking to former scholarship athletes, I found them to be significantly less involved with other extracurriculars on campus. Their sport was their primary (and in many instances, sole) extracurricular activity. This doesn't make D-I or D-III better or worse than the other. It does, however, make the experiences very different.

My professional experiences are largely based on the extremes, but there are also hundreds and hundreds of options at the D-II (both scholarship and non-scholarship, NAIA, and junior college levels. If you know what you want, your needs can be met by a great academic institution and a great coaching staff.

You have to be honest with yourself about how much of your college experience you want to devote to your sport. You also have to be honest with yourself about how strong your time management skills are, and whether or not you are motivated enough to improve them. Ask yourself, "regardless of the competitive level I choose, am I ready to essentially have a side-job while I am also a college student?"

What are your deal-breakers or makers when it comes to a college campus?

For this subject, I want you to imagine that you're a great fit for a specific team and coaching staff. What else would that college need to look like for you to want to go there? Similarly, what would make that environment a deal-breaker for you? Ask yourself the following questions, at an absolute minimum:

- Do I want to go to a large or small school?
- Do I want to go to a public or private school?
- Do I want to go to a college where standardized tests are optional for admissions?
- Do I want to be in a larger city?
- Do I want to attend a faith-based school?
- Do I want to attend an all-male or all-female school?
- Do I want to live on campus while I attend school?
- Do I like the mission of the school?

The above questions are by no means comprehensive, but they should get your noggin churning about your preferred environment.

How important is NIL/scholarship money to my family and I?

No two families approach college selection on the same footing, and family finances may play a major factor in your college decision. If so, there are a few things you should know.

The spiraling cost of college has made an athletic scholarship seem like the only pathway to higher education for some. At D-I and D-II levels, athletic scholarships are an option. But there are other options you may not be aware of.

Many colleges offer merit scholarships, based on the quality of your high school grades. NCAA D-III schools are not permitted to offer athletic scholarships, but many offer academic merit money as a recruiting tool. There are also tons of grants and scholarships that you can apply for independently that may help fund your college experience. There are also hundreds of academically-selective colleges that purposefully admit students who "meet demonstrated financial need" in order to bring in the most diverse admissions class possible. These institutions exist in some capacity at every level of athletic competition, but are most commonly seen at the D-III level. In these instances, from the information you provide on your federal financial aid application, the college calculates how much money your family is expected to contribute. If you get in, you owe what the aid calculator says you can afford, ranging from nothing to everything.

Scholarships and merit money aside, the field of intercollegiate athletics has recently experienced major breakthroughs regarding NIL compensation. Athletes can now be compensated by boosters, or sign endorsement deals based on their name, image, and likeness. If this is important to you, you should mention it to the coaches recruiting you.

How are your grades?

Confession time. I was a stinker in high school! I had a GPA of barely 2.0 halfway through my sophomore year. I didn't apply myself in subjects I wasn't good at, I hated homework, and I had a documented reading comprehension learning disability which led me to avoid reading at all costs. I weirdly turned into an avid reader later in life, and now I'm writing a book. Isn't life interesting?

I was more interested in talking about sports than doing school work. So, on days I wasn't with friends after school, I'd call into the local drive time sports radio show, "Wally and the Keeg" on 1050 ESPN Radio. I'd consistently lie about my age and, if the screener was generous enough, I'd get on the air and stumble through a pre-written rant. It was glorious!

A key mentor of mine was my high school guidance counselor, Nori Cerny. I will NEVER forget my sophomore year winter check in with her. She knew I wanted to be a sports broadcaster, and she sat me down to review the profiles of a bunch of professional broadcasters. All of them had attended a four-year college and obtained a degree of some kind. Point blank, Miss Cerny said to me, "If this is what you want to do, you need to get your grades up and you need to go to college.

I know you can do this, and you need to stop messing around. You're a good kid, just do the work."

By the time I was halfway through my senior year, my GPA had jumped to a 3.28. For most places, however, that was too little, too late. I did manage to get into one college. With the help of a generous admissions liaison in Miss Cerny's network, I was admitted to Quinnipiac University. A member of their hockey team showed me around campus on admitted students' day. I fell in love. The undergrad experience I had there was phenomenal, but it nearly didn't happen because I didn't have my act together. This may seem obvious, but if you want to be a college athlete… YOU HAVE TO GET INTO COLLEGE.

The NCAA, NJCAA, and NAIA all have eligibility centers and compliance centers available online where you can create a profile to best navigate the recruiting process at the level(s) of your choice. They discuss the academic criteria you need to meet in high school to be eligible to compete. At certain competitive divisions, the eligibility centers yield to the academic requirements of each individual college or university. The more prestigious the school, the harder it is to get in.

I firmly believe in the value of a college degree, along with the critical thinking skills that come with it, so I would advocate for you to attend the most academically prestigious college or university that a) you can get into and b) makes financial sense for your family. If you want to earn a spot as a college athlete, you need to be eligible. In addition to athletes meeting eligibility, several coaches I spoke to review athletes' grades to determine if they can balance the rigor of being college students and college athletes at the same time. These students may have been eligible according to the rules, but they still had to pass the eye test of an experienced coach. In short, your grades don't just tell the story of your ability to learn. They indicate your ability to balance. Utilize this time to build a plan for yourself to develop and/or maintain good study habits. You will need them later.

I've done some soul searching and I feel good about my grades and my academic plan. What's next?

Now it's time for a test drive. Start looking up schools that interest you. Tour different college campuses in your region. Get a feel for which types of campuses you vibe with. If you're super new to this process, you don't even need to interact with a coaching staff. Just walk around some campuses and get a feel for them. If you are thinking heavily about going the AAU/Club route and have not found a program yet, this is also a great time to try and find one that matches your values. You can ask program directors about their team's mission, their style of play, and how many players in their program aspire to play collegiately. The next chapter is focused on mentorship, and delves into how important it is.

Game and Highlight Film

This is also the time to start compiling game film. You'll want to start working on two separate projects. One is a highlight reel, and one is a full game film.

NAIL THE RECRUITING PROCESS

We'll start with your full game film, because that is easier. Your goal should be to capture as many of your full games on film as possible. The games you send to coaches should meet two specific criteria. First, you should be playing against great competition. Second, you should feel really good about the way you played in that game.

The number of points you individually scored does not matter as much as the quality of your all-around play against good competition. It doesn't matter if you scored 47 points in a basketball game if it was against a terrible team! To drive this point home, several of my personal favorites—on film and in-person—were games in which the prospect I was recruiting actually lost the game! What stood out was their outstanding individual effort and how they led their team the best they could.

Whenever possible, try to submit a full game film where the audio can be heard clearly. It's great if a coach can hear you communicating on the floor. Background music should not be included.

Your highlight film should be your "best of" reel, be less than ten minutes in length, and feature a variety of your skills. I'd recommend that your highlight film also include a title page in the beginning that includes your name, the team you play for, your jersey number, and your basic stats if you have access to them.

For a basketball player, these stats would include points, rebounds or assists depending on position, and percentages. I really value the FT% stat being on the title page because then you don't have to include video of you making free throws in your highlight reel. Your title page will be followed by video of you making your best plays for your team on both sides of the ball. Highlight film can also be customizable. It's your chance to further differentiate yourself. If you consider yourself a tough defensive player, and have video of you diving for loose balls and taking charges, I promise you that film is more valuable to a coach than footage of you making your 6th or 7th jump shot.

The more versatile your game is, the better it looks to a coach. They will notice if every basket you make on your highlight tape comes off a right handed drive with a right handed finish. Review your own highlight tape by watching it as if you were a coach. Are all of your makes coming from the same spot on the floor? Does the film show a limitation that you may not have been aware of? Look for any clips of you doing the same thing and try to replace them with something different. Don't have something different? Well, now you're aware of what you need to work on!

A lot of athletes elect to include background music in their highlight tapes. This is by no means required. If you choose to do it, please be sure that the music does not contain profanity. Profanity laced music in your highlight tape is a huge red flag.

How do I know if I'm ready to be recruited?

Unfortunately, you don't. But you can be aware of what the sweet spot in the process looks like. Standard recruiting relationships tend to begin in your sophomore and junior years of high school. There can be exceptions, and I'm sure you've heard stories about the random 8th graders who got high level Division I scholarship offers, but you don't need to panic if that is not you. Your goal is to have your GEAR ready by the middle of your high school career. While there are plenty of success stories of athletes who developed their GEAR later, they had to act with a heightened sense of urgency. If you aren't being contacted by college coaches by the mid-point of your high school career, you need to start initiating correspondence with them (more on this correspondence in chapter 5).

I know there is a lot to process in this chapter. But remember, we are focusing right now on developing your awareness. Take the necessary time to do it now and you can prioritize your growth by deploying this knowledge to accelerate your next steps. When you're ready, it's time to find your mentors.

FOR PARENTS/GUARDIANS:

There are two really important areas where you can assist your child in this chapter. We'll start with the simpler of the two.

1) If your child's high school or AAU team does not already record their games... well... congratulations on your new volunteer position! For about 50 bucks you can buy a tripod for your phone and record them, then upload the footage to Google Drive for free. Don't want to use your phone? No worries. You can get a cheap tablet and use that as your video recorder. Can you pay for a service to do this? Sure, but you definitely don't need to. PRO TIP: During breaks in the game, move the camera to the scoreboard so anyone watching can know what is going on. You capturing the video will take a

lot of stress off your child's plate. You can also work as a team to edit it down into a highlight film using the free software available on tablets, Macs, and PCs. Again, you do not need to hire a service for this.

Here's an analogy that can help you distill all that content into a stunning highlight film for your child - it is a cover letter. Full game film is a resume. Try and guide your child accordingly when it comes to editing.

2) Now for the less simple stuff. I've been using the word "child" on purpose. They are amazing young people, but they are also not yet fully cognitively developed. There are still going to be some areas where you may know your child better than they know themselves. For example, if your child articulates to you that they want to go to a large school for college, but you know your child gets overwhelmed around a lot of people, now is the time to challenge them on that notion.

Ultimately, every parent wants their child to make the best decisions for themselves, but children don't always do that. That's why working on awareness is so important. Use this time to challenge them to think critically not only about what they want, but also about their past experiences and how these experiences made them feel. These types of conversations are not only helpful now, but also will help shape future conversations as you shift from decision makers to consultants for your child.

SECTION 2

GROW

FINDING YOUR MENTORS

I would not be where I am today without incredible mentors.

Last chapter, I shared a mentoring experience I had with Miss Cerny. Now, I want to talk briefly about another mentor, Dr. Lisa Burns. She was one of several amazing professors I had at Quinnipiac University, and we formed a closer relationship because she supervised my senior thesis about how athletes from different racial backgrounds are portrayed in broadcasts and advertisements.

After gathering really interesting data from surveys and interviews with both sports fans and sports media personalities, I got so excited to write that I pulled an all-nighter and wrote the entire thing in one shot, despite the fact that it wasn't due for another three weeks. Through bloodshot eyes, I submitted a self-edited thesis to Professor Burns digitally, and went to bed as my roommates left for classes that morning. This was quintessential college Jared. Energy forward and passionate about projects, but also the least patient college student in the universe, with a knack for missing details. When I woke up from my nap, I had an email from Dr. Burns asking me to meet in person. Attached to the email was a series of edits, along with a comment at the end: "I can't accept this paper. You know you're better than this."

The paper was plagued with spelling, grammar, and punctuation mistakes. I also had multiple sections that barely made sense. As soon as my adrenaline wore off, I realized that the work I submitted was mostly garbage. Our meeting went about as you'd expect, and I found Dr. Burns to be incredibly motivating in her honesty. I was shocked by how patient she was with me, but she still made it clear that she'd chosen to supervise my thesis work because she knew what I was capable of, and that what'd I'd submitted simply wasn't it.

I spent the following two weeks working on that paper, completely rewriting several sections of it. At the end of that semester, I won Quinnipiac's 2008 Student Achievement in Media Studies award. This is firmly one of my favorite memories.

When I was introduced as the recipient of that award, the Dean of the School of Communications, David Donnelly, proclaimed that I had gotten a tattoo of a radio microphone on my left arm inspired by our college radio station, 98.1 WQAQ. This was true. It was also true that I had successfully hidden that tattoo from my dad until then, and that was how he found out.

Whoops.

… Anywho, Dr. Burns was a great mentor to me, and all great mentors have one specific thing in common: They coach you, whether you're prepared for it or not.

I got coached by Dr. Burns to dig deeper, work harder, and apply myself to the best of my abilities, and at the end I received an award for it! You might have good resources at your disposal, but there is a difference between a resource and a mentor. A mentor is always prepared to challenge you with the truth, because they trust you are capable of responding to it in a positive way. Great coaches are great mentors. And in order to find a great mentor at the next level, you need a great mentor right now.

Based on the insight of the athletes I spoke to; I actually think you need two great mentors right now.

Mentor #1: A Coaching Mentor

There is a chance that you already have a coach in your sport that you consider a mentor. If so, great! If not, here is what you need to know.

The basketball players I interviewed all stressed how important it was to them that they had a mentor, with knowledge of college basketball, in their corner. This mentor challenged them on the court and helped them develop as players, but also offered them guidance and honesty off the court as they tried to narrow down their list of college choices. For some, that mentor was an AAU coach. For others, it was a high school coach. Some also found third party mentors outside of their teams that included skills trainers, scouting services or coordinators, and advisors like me. When it comes to finding a mentor, there are tons of right answers and really only one wrong answer. If someone is in your circle, in a position of influence, and they are not offering you productive feedback that encourages further growth, they are NOT your mentor.

Please take a moment to really process that.

This doesn't mean you should sign up to be demeaned by a mentor! And you can usually tell if someone isn't fit to mentor you by how they treat others close to them. You don't need a mentor to put you down, but you do need radical honesty from them. Here are a few examples of mentorship from my interviews.

One player had a mentor tell them to cross certain schools off their list because of fit concerns.

Another had a mentor talk them out of going to a college's "elite" camps because they didn't think that specific college was actually interested in them.

A third athlete is a player I've known since they started high school. This athlete shared a story of their AAU coach dividing their program into two teams. The first consisted of players the coach assessed as athletic scholarship ready. The second comprised players the coach thought would be more successful at the non-scholarship level. This athlete told me that a lot of conflict erupted in the wake of this decision, particularly from the parents of players placed on the second team. But the coach stuck with their gut decision, and nearly everyone on both teams was placed where the coach predicted they would be. Not a single player from the second team received a D-I scholarship offer. At the time these athletes received this information, it was likely hard to digest. This doesn't make it any less true or important. A mentor has the courage to share truth with a mentee, regardless of consequence.

Beyond how they handle you and your family, you should also evaluate a mentor on their expertise. Find a mentor who has a deep understanding of the collegiate competitive level you want to play at.

When I recruit a prospect, I usually talk to their coaching mentor multiple times. Those conversations tend to go best when the mentor is either a former college athlete, or a former college coach. The reason is simple: they get it. They know what coaches are actually looking for, and they know what it takes to compete at the next level.

In my time coaching, I have also encountered a number of coaches and services at the high school level that are unwilling to be as honest with recruits and their families as they should be. Unfortunately, these are also the types of people that tend to be very good at selling themselves. Here's an example of that.

One of the CCQ coaches was coming off the best season in the history of their program when they told me about a recent conversation with a high school recruit's mentor. The mentor thought the player was flying under the radar as a recruit. During the conversation, the mentor insisted that their player would be a great fit for the coach's offensive system. The coach replied by asking the mentor if they had ever actually watched that team play to know if their player was a great fit. The mentor said no. I could say a lot about that, but in short, that player did not find the right mentor.

If you are still looking for an AAU or club team, it is important to find one that meets you where you are, and provides you the right mentorship to move you forward. If you are dead set on being a scholarship athlete, you can find a program with mentors that can serve the accompanying needs. Similarly, I know of several organizations that specialize in placing athletes with the right fit for them, regardless of competitive level. Remember, the data suggests that AAU/club sports were most effective when providing players with mentorship and visibility to college coaches. Those should be your two most important criteria when making this decision.

Here is a great practice you can use to filter and find the right mentor. First, share existing game film and highlight film with your prospective mentor. Then—*especially if your potential mentor is a trainer*—attend a training session with them. Let them evaluate you and gauge them for honesty. If they do not talk to you about any limitations at all, cross them off your list. If it's all shiny and golden and praise, it's all fake.

Please keep in mind that your mentor is exactly that, YOURS. You get to decide their level of involvement in your process. And, depending on your personality, you will use your mentor differently than others may use theirs. One player I spoke to only utilized their mentor to make the initial match with a college coaching staff. It was important to them that they facilitated all future correspondence afterwards so coaches knew they were a relationship-oriented recruit. This is a great practice, but there are also some players who utilize their mentors to talk to college coaches about the progress they've been making and how their recruiting process is going. This is also a great practice.

There's no right way to use a mentor's guidance. There's just the right guidance, and you definitely need it. By engaging with a strong coaching mentor, you will gain a more accurate focus on where you need to grow, while also knowing you will be supported in that growth.

Mentor #2: A Player Mentor

I asked every player I interviewed who had transferred from their original college to identify differences in their earlier and later recruiting processes. While their replies differed in terms of certain tactics, their responses all shared one specific theme. The second time around, the questions they all asked were more specific and intentional. They also had a better gauge of which coaching staffs' responses were the most genuine.

These comments, combined with my data around the average recruits' readiness for college sports, informed my use of the word "Aware" in the GEAR acronym. In the interest of building this specific category of awareness, you owe it to yourself to find a second mentor.

The criteria for mentor #2 is a little more specific. First, they have to be a current or former college athlete in your desired sport. Second, they have to be no more than 10 years older than you.

The first point is easy enough to explain. If you reach out to an alum of your varsity or club team, you are reaching out to someone who previously lived your current experience and currently lives your dream. They can shed light by sharing their experience and reflecting on the things they wish they'd known sooner. Even if you plan to go to a college on the opposite side of the planet from this person, you can still take their advice and use it in your process.

What about the age part? Well…

I recently asked a player what their favorite classic rock band was, and they said the "Red Hot Chili Peppers." In addition to breaking me emotionally, this response taught me one very important thing about the players I coach: we aren't from the same time.

A limitation of some mentors is that they do not appreciate the lens through which you see the world. They don't get your world because they are not living in it. In your world, mumble rap is a good genre of music. In my world, we use the phrase "genre of music," so we certainly don't like mumble rap.

There's a saying in college coaching that describes new players upon arrival: "They don't know what they don't know." I agree with the basic sentiment of the phrase, but I actually think it deserves to be expanded. When it comes to the recruiting process, college coaches don't know what you don't know either. A college coach is so wrapped up in their program and the day-to-day management of it that they often forget how drastically different their players' lives are to the lives of high schoolers. If you don't know what to ask a college coach, or

NAIL THE RECRUITING PROCESS

don't have a real view of the day-to-day from your player mentor, you're just as likely to get caught off guard by the parts of this experience that may not have even been withheld from you intentionally. There is no one that can help you frame and then answer your current questions and concerns better than a current or recent college athlete. And if you don't get a potential player mentor nailed down immediately, it becomes an opportunity to keep working on engaging.

In the next section of the book, you're going to start cold emailing coaches. If that idea makes you nervous, then you should practice on a player mentor. Remember, these are young people who are working with teams and practicing servant leadership every day. They'll likely be excited to help you! And with the vast number of college athletes on social media, you have endless mentorship options.

Shoot for the moon. How dope would it be if you messaged one of your favorite local players, and they became your player mentor? I can't guarantee it will happen, but you might as well try. The more you practice engaging with potential mentors now, the more comfortable you'll be engaging later in the process. Try something as simple as sending a DM to an athlete. Introduce yourself and share how you aspire to play the same sport collegiately, and would love to learn more about their experience. The worst case scenario is that they don't respond. That's okay, it just means they weren't meant to be your mentor! Try the next one. This is a "shoot until you score" sort of exercise.

Once you have your mentors in place, you can act on their feedback. This loop of engagement and awareness will drive you into the next two chapters, because now it's time to double down on growth.

FOR PARENTS/GUARDIANS:

Your job is to help your child find a mentor match. Let's say your child is dead set on competing at the high-academic D-III level, but their mentor has no D-III network or experience. That's not to say your child can't still get great information from this mentor, but it might not be the right information for them. Conversely, let's say your child is dead set on playing at the JUCO level for two years to gauge their college readiness. You can find a mentor that has worked with previous JUCO players and obtain a player mentor that currently or formerly played at a JUCO. This would be a perfect mentor match that provides the perfect information.

Your child is going to meet people in this process who are going to be great, but not necessarily aligned with what they actually need. As an adult, you are better equipped to identify this and talk to your child about it. There are tons of great mentors out there. Do some reference checks. Help your child make sure it's the right match.

GROWING YOUR NETWORK

The next two chapters are going to be presented one after the other... because that's just how books work... but in practice, you're going to want to execute what you learn in both of these chapters at the same time.

CHARTING YOUR PATH

For a moment, I want you to again visualize recruiting from the perspective of a college coach. While the smaller details of recruiting can differ from staff to staff, there tend to be four major steps to a recruiting cycle.

1) Identify talent
2) Build a relationship
3) Build interest, if there's a fit
4) Close the deal and get the young talent on their team

Coaches tend to repeat these four steps until they have accomplished their penultimate goal of matriculating the best recruiting class possible. Now, let's take those four major steps and reverse engineer them so they're tailored to your goal...

1) Identify schools that are an ideal fit
2) Build a relationship with the coaches at those schools
3) Narrow your choices and build continued interest with your top 3-5 schools
4) Make an informed decision

If you're using this book as a guide, you're currently somewhere between steps 1 and 2. That means it's time to start reaching out to coaches. Everyone has varying levels of comfort when it comes to interpersonal engagement with authority figures, especially for younger people. So, I get it if the thought of picking up the phone to speak to a college coach makes your palms sweat.

But don't panic! Coaches are people too. Plus, they're in the business of relationship building, so they'll likely be more welcoming than the typical authority figure.

Each recruiting process is going to be a little different, depending on your level of exposure to the coach. For the sake of simplicity, let's say you have never been contacted by a college coach and need to start networking from scratch. Your big goal is to get a coach on the phone with you. To get there, you'll take the following steps.

1) IDENTIFY TARGET COACHES TO ENGAGE WITH

Based on your original values search (from Section 1 of this book) there may already be some schools you're interested in. Build on that list by utilizing your guidance counselor, as well as resources online, to help find more schools that match your interests.

From there, it's time to start looking up staffs. Take your time with this step. Really be sure to get as much information as you can. Try to learn where coaches came from, what their philosophies are, and do some Google and YouTube searches for interviews with them. In addition to helping you confirm a fit, this will help inform the content of your discussions with them. No one likes repeating themselves, and you want to ask questions that are unique to you.

In terms of who on a staff to reach out to, I don't really think there is a wrong answer. Just know that at the higher levels of competition, you'll encounter head coaches with more support staff. That means your correspondence may be forwarded to an assistant coach.

Head coaches tend to structure their staffs in certain ways that streamline recruiting correspondence. For example, at the D-I level, I was in charge of developing our team's guards. If our head coach got an email from a guard, she would often forward that email to me to help evaluate the content.

With this in mind, you should target whoever you can access. If you follow a certain assistant coach and they follow you back on social media, that's a great access point. You can also go on a college's website and search their staff directory for a coach's email address to gain another access point.

2) INITIAL OUTREACH

Once you have enough access points, you'll draft your initial outreach. Remember the goal here - you are not asking all your questions and bombarding them in this initial outreach! You will be using your initial outreach to ultimately get on the phone with a coach. To earn that call, you are going to implement a method that combines text messages, DMs, and emails. Here is what you will need (in no specific order):

1) A dedicated email address to your recruiting process (free and easy)
2) An APPROPRIATE social media page, at a minimum on Instagram (free and easy)
3) An unofficial copy of your most current academic transcript (free and easy)
4) A YouTube page or dedicated public Google Drive folder that has your highlight and game film (free and easy)

First Step: Comb through your Instagram page to gauge the appropriateness of its content. Your parents can help with this (parents see the section devoted to you for more guidance on this). Once it passes your eye test, change your profile/bio to include your full name, high school team, and club/AAU team (if applicable). Make sure your profile/bio has a few links to your game film and team schedules.

IMPORTANT NOTE: While some coaches I spoke to were more patient with inappropriate social media content, others identified inappropriate social media posts as glaring "red flags" that could potentially end their relationship with the recruit who posted it. Examples of inappropriate content included, but were not limited to, posts featuring illegal substances (including alcohol being consumed underage), posts with foul language, and memes/re-posts containing racist/sexist/homophobic content.

Second Step: Assuming you do not have a coach's cell phone number to text them, follow them on Instagram (coaches leverage Instagram a lot in recruiting, so trust they'll be there). You then want to send them a DM to briefly—*BRIEFLY*—introduce yourself. Let them know you are interested in their school and that you would like to learn more about their program by phone. Include a link to your highlight and game film in this DM. End the message by instructing them to look out for an email from your email address, then thank them for their time and interest. If you do have their cell phone number, you can text this instead. Either medium works. Just be sure to include your Instagram handle in the text message so they can look you up.

EXAMPLE:

> Coach Jared,
>
> My name is (your name). I'm a 6'1" sophomore point guard currently playing for Bayside High Schcol in New York and the Ultimate Elite AAU program. I'm very interested in attending (their university) and would like to set up a time to talk by phone so we can learn more about one another. I've copied a link to my AAU highlight reel and some full

game film against strong competition. Also, be on the lookout for an email from abc123@whatever.com containing more information. Thank you so much for your time, and I look forward to hearing back from you!

-Your name

Third Step: Using the email address you found in the staff directory, send an email to the same coach you just DMed or texted. This email can follow the same beats of your text, but should include more details. Your email should also be proofread and free of grammatical and spelling errors.

EXAMPLE:

Coach Jared,

My name is (your name), and I am writing as a follow up to the message I sent you earlier.

I am very interested in becoming a member of the Athlete University basketball program, where I think I can be a strong fit both athletically and academically. I'm a point guard that plays in a similar system at Bayside High School, and I think our coaching staff is doing a great job preparing me for the style of play at Athlete U. I've heard amazing things about your school's architecture program, have always wanted to go to school in a big city, and think I could be a great fit at Athlete U.

NAIL THE RECRUITING PROCESS

I just completed my sophomore season. We made it to the sectional semifinal and were eliminated by the eventual sectional champion. It was a disappointing finish, but my teammates and I are already looking forward to next season. This summer, I will be playing AAU basketball with the Ultimate Elite. See attached for our schedule so you know what events we will be at.

In addition to contact information for my coaches, I have also included my highlight tape from this season as well as full game film of that sectional semifinal game. Despite having lost, it was a great game against a team that also has a number of players looking to play college basketball at schools like Athlete U.

If you are interested in me as a recruit, I would love to set up a time to talk on the phone. Please feel free to email or text me to let me know what times could work for you.

Thanks so much again for your time and attention.

Sincerely,

(Your name)
(Your phone number and email address)

IMPORTANT NOTE ABOUT EMAILS

Two pivotal things have changed about email since the time I started coaching:

1) A number of paid services have come out that allow you to automate emails to coaches.
2) The recruiting process has shifted away from emails, with texts and DMs becoming more common means of communication.

I do not believe these two things are merely coincidental. It has happened to us all as increasingly more marketing and robotic emails have clogged up our inboxes. And just like the rest of us, coaches and recruits alike have been less inclined to open emails that don't look like they were written by a real person. Therefore, I consider it MANDATORY that you take the extra time to customize each individual email. Yes, that is a lot of work. And yes, this will be a huge differentiator for you in this process, and will also help prepare you for a college environment that will see you receiving multiple crucial emails daily that are easy to miss. So write your own emails, and get into the habit of checking your email twice a day.

Remember, being a college athlete is going to take tremendous extra work on your part, both on and off the court, field, or track. Illustrating that you are able to put in that extra work now can be a separator in your process.

The Response Window

There is such a thing as overdoing it when it comes to communication. And there are some coaches that are guilty of this too. I think a good sweet spot is five business days before following up. If a coach has not replied to you in five business days, you can send that follow up text or email you've been itching to send. It can literally say, "Just following up to see if you got my previous email, which I've copied below." You can then paste the email and be on your way. In another five business days, you can either drop it and move on, or attempt to reach out to a different coach on staff.

Did you react negatively to my suggestion that you drop it and move on? Well then, I want you to consider something... coaches are *flooded* with emails, calls, and texts about potential recruits. While it's not a great practice, some coaches don't respond to all of their emails as a time and sanity saving measure. If they don't think you're a good fit, they may not tell you.

I hate that it works that way, but the best thing you can do is just consider it a miss. In sports, you miss more than you hit. The best athletes still miss the majority of the time. Resilience is built by attempts. Keep trying.

The Phone Call

You've worked really hard to reach this moment, and now you're about to be on the phone with a member of a college coaching staff. Conversations are meant to be organic, so I don't have a rigid structure for you here. But I do have a list of best practices.

Here's… insert awesome blaring trumpet sounds… THE PHONE CALL PREP LIST.

1) You are ready to share your awareness

As coaches are generally aiming to learn more about you, there are several standard questions they tend to ask. In order to best answer them, you need to lean on your awareness areas. Be ready to share:

a) What you are interested in academically
b) Your preferred style of play
c) Your preferred style of coaching
d) Your strengths as a player/teammate
e) Your areas of improvement as a player/teammate
f) What interests you about their specific school and team

Think the above sounds simple? Well, you'd be floored by the number of coaches who think this self-awareness is both critically important to early conversations and often missing in phone calls. The more you clearly articulate who you are and what you want, the more likely a coach is to reflect positively on the conversation.

When it comes to awareness, the CCQ expects a recruit they are pursuing to be able to accurately articulate their own strengths and limitations (7). Consider it a self-awareness check. If you followed the steps in the book, then the coach you're speaking to already watched your film and they now want to make sure you know yourself.

2) You are the opposite of a dud

I'm probably dating myself by using the word "dud." Hey, you should be thankful I haven't pulled out any early 90s sitcom references yet.

In real life, a dud describes a bomb that lands but never actually detonates. In conversation, a dud is a person who gives one word responses and then stops talking, even when met with excitement and energy.

If you're a dud on the phone, it can be a deal breaker... so CUT...IT...OUT (nailed the reference).

The best way to de-dud your behavior is to answer every question like it's an open ended question rather than a simple yes or no closed question, even if it is one. Coaches with more experience are great at asking open ended questions, like "How do you like to be coached?" instead of "Do you respond well to this style of coaching?" The first of those questions is open and therefore invites a longer response, but you can answer the second with more than a yes or no.

There's no guarantee you'll always get an open ended question, so your job is to find a way to answer both types of questions the same way. Think about your awareness areas, use examples of experiences that culminated in that awareness, and answer honestly. The more quality content in your response, the more likely the coach is to extend the conversation. It's all about sharing.

This process is designed to help you find the best fit, and the odds are high that not every coach you talk to will also be that. The more you engage, the more you learn. Remember the engagement related data from earlier in the book? Coaches tend to evaluate recruits based on their level of engagement with them in conversations. Be engaging. Don't be a dud.

3) You have prepared a growth-oriented question bank

Most coaches will also treat introductory conversations as a venue to answer some of your questions. Near the end of an introductory conversation, a coach will usually ask you if you have any questions.

I am now going to let you in on a secret that will prepare you for both recruiting, and the rest of your adult life. This is a loaded question. There is a correct answer. The correct answer is, "yes, I have a few questions."

If anyone in any conversation or interview asks you if you have any questions for them, it means they are expecting you to. Furthermore, they expect that your questions show some level of critical thinking. I couldn't tell you in a million years why it works this way, but it does. It was clear that the majority of the CCQ expected recruits to have questions—and good ones—for them. So, if you're going to have to ask good questions then you might as well ask them in a way that helps you gauge a coach's authenticity.

NAIL THE RECRUITING PROCESS

Below is a bank of great introductory questions that either a) have been directly asked of me by a recruit or b) were recommended by one of the players I interviewed. My advice would be to choose any two of them and ask them. Then ask the final question on this list. The final question is mandatory (more on this next chapter).

Make note of your questions, and also take notes of how the coaches responded. Listen critically, not only for the words they used, but for the words they didn't. In some of your conversations, a coach will say things that really resonate with you. In others, not so much. These notes will help steer you towards the right fit. Keep track of them.

a) Can you tell me what you're specifically looking for in my year's recruiting class?
b) I noticed that your preferred style of play is (insert their style of play here). How do you see me fitting into that?
c) I'd like to (insert what you want to do professionally, or insert that you have no idea what you want to do professionally) after I graduate. Can you talk to me about the path towards that at your school?
d) Can you tell me about your team's culture and environment?
e) Last season, your team (insert how their team finished here). What would you say their strengths were, and where does your team need to improve?
f) How do you think your players would describe you as a coach?

g) How do you handle "tough" conversations with players? For example, conversations about playing time or commitment levels.
h) Can you share what you feel differentiates you and your staff from other programs out there?
i) Based on what you've seen from my play, what can I work on to be more prepared to compete at your level?

Repeat. Repeat. Repeat.

Repeat the steps in this chapter over and over until you are satisfied with the pool of coaches from different schools you have spoken to. As you build these relationships, many coaching staffs will rotate their conversations with you so that everyone gets to know you. Take full advantage of this. Consider asking multiple staff members the same questions to see if they share common philosophies and answers. That can be really important when it comes to gauging staff consistency and transparency.

Prospect Clinics and Camps

The two most conventional ways of getting on a coach's radar are you reaching out to them after learning about them, or them reaching out to you after watching you play. But there is a third option, and it is one that has become exponentially more popular amongst college coaches over the last decade or so.

Over the course of my coaching career, I have offered dozens of roster spots to players that I coached at an elite camp, a showcase camp or a prospect clinic. The kicker is that, in many of those instances, I had not previously evaluated that player in person. Tons of recruits fly under the radar like that, and some coaching staffs use camps to try and find them.

As a D-III coach, I intentionally worked at D-I elite camps and regional academic showcase camps. At the D-I level, we hosted elite and team camps where we evaluated anyone who we thought might have the potential to compete at that level. Several CCQ coaches told me they actually preferred finding recruits at camps as opposed to the standard recruiting method. Why? Camps gave them an opportunity to see how an athlete directly responded to their coaching. A solid camp performance under a college coach's supervision could greatly differentiate you from your peers.

Utilize your mentoring network to assess some camps where you could stand out. These could be high academic camps, elite camps at a specific college, or camps put on by independent agencies that are staffed and monitored by college players and coaches.

FOR PARENTS/GUARDIANS:

Your level of involvement in the material covered in this chapter will depend largely on your child's level of conversational comfort. That said, even if your child is on the shy side, I would still encourage you to take as much of a preparatory role as possible. This will include social media, email, and phone calls.

For starters, if your child has active social media accounts, you MUST follow their accounts with zero restrictions or "mutes." You'll then get to see everything they post so you can potentially protect them from a misfire. Please note that you are NOT posting things for them.

As for texts and emails, you can help proofread messages and emails and ensure that they're sending concise, cohesive messages. But again, please note that you are NOT drafting or sending emails for them.

You can also do a lot to help your child with phone prep, especially if your child gets nervous talking to new people. Do a mock call with them, so they can practice articulating their responses. Assess these responses. The more comfortable they get, the better they'll eventually do on the phone. But… you've guessed it… please note that you are NOT talking to a coach for them.

Notice a pattern here?

There is a fine line between helping your child prepare, and you doing the work for them. Do not cross that line. No matter how eager you are to see your child succeed and even if it makes things quicker or more efficient in the moment, it will become problematic down the road.

Let's flash forward to the fall of your child's first year of college. You do not want to set your child up for an experience where a coach or authority figure on campus needs something from them, and your child all of a sudden doesn't sound the same. I've seen it happen. It's painful to watch, let alone experience! Any line-crossing efforts you make now may limit your child's ability to find the correct fit later.

As you advance in the recruiting process, coaches will converse more deeply with you and ask meaningful questions. When asked, please feel free to give your honest opinion about your child. But look, for your child's sake, it's important to get to that point organically. The data suggests there are many coaches who would consider ending a relationship with a recruit because of their over involved parents. Of course you know way more about your child than a coach would… but you also need to know the difference between speaking about your child, and speaking for your child.

GROWING YOUR GAME

We're about to dive into a chapter devoted to teaching you ways to improve as a young athlete. Before we do so, there's something you need to know.

The Growth Disclaimer

As you focus on growth, you will find that some parts of your skill set are harder to grow than others. This is going to make you uncomfortable.

You will likely feel compelled to cut corners and take shortcuts in these areas. I know this because I did not magically travel to age 37 using a time machine. When I was your age, I didn't value growth the way I should have. Any time I really put 100% into something and cut absolutely zero corners, I did it while gritting my teeth and thinking that it was unnecessary. I only realized how important those moments actually were at the tail end of college.

I'm begging you to learn quicker than I did.

Here's one great thing about sports - they really are the last true meritocracy out there. You get something because you've earned it. You earn trust, you earn minutes, and you earn your reputation. You give more, you get more.

Here's another great thing about sports (even though you may not think this is great at your current age) - when you do cut corners, your teammates and coaches notice. And the best teammates and coaches will call you out on it.

The more you visibly cut corners after being called out, the less inclined a college coach or teammate is to continue working with you. They'll still be your supporters, sure, but they won't challenge you as much. And in a team sport, they can usually replace you with someone else that will not cut corners.

So if you find yourself gritting your teeth or feeling compelled to cut a corner during this chapter, remember this: if you want to be successful at the next level, you're going to have to go all-in. You might as well start now and build that habit. Run your race, don't compare yourself to your peers. Just focus on growing you.

If you remain unconvinced, please read through this chapter anyway. I promise that you're going to see some data at the end that will reel you back in.

Ready? Here we go.

ASSESS YOUR GAME

Remember the one question last chapter that was mandatory? That's where we're going to start. Make note of the areas in which a college coach thinks you should improve, then start brainstorming ways to do that in a workout.

An interesting personal note on that question: I would say 90% of the time I was asked that question, and I answered honestly, I would hear a response to the effect of "my current coach has told me that too." The odds are that you already know at least some of what you need to work on, and you've just been ducking it. You can't escape your limitations when it comes to sports. The real winners are those willing to tackle them.

I am intentionally not going to use this space to give you a bank of drills, because I am not currently coaching you, but I will tell you this: Your work should be built entirely around the feedback you are getting from your mentors and the college coaches you've spoken to.

At the collegiate level, I consistently see one specific behavior that limits potential. The average athlete will be made aware of the areas for growth in their game… then continue to spend most of their time working on something else that they're already good at. The average athlete—and person in general—will tend to stay in their comfort zone during individual or un-supervised workouts. That's the easy thing to do. I am asking you to do the hard thing. Work on the things you need to work on, even if it frustrates you. That's how you grow.

The Best Coach in the World

If you have a coach or trainer that can help you develop your skills, great! Set up a couple of weekly sessions with them in your off-season. Let them guide you. If you don't have access to that, you have nothing to worry about. Why? Because you're wrong. You have access to the best coach in the world - the internet.

Search engines and YouTube are home to hundreds of thousands of hours of drill work, skill work, and coaching points for every sport imaginable. There are also a growing number of apps in both the free and paid spaces that can help customize full workouts for you based on what you submit as your areas of improvement.

Here is an example of how much content is available. Let's say you are a right hand dominant basketball player and know you need to improve dribbling skills with your left hand. Consider yourself in luck, because I just entered the query "drills to improve weak dribbling hand" into Google and got 1.48 million results, including more than 46,000 instructional YouTube videos.

Workout Hits

A successful workout is a combination of what you plan to do and how you execute it. Here's a checklist to make sure you have it down.

YOU ARE INTENTIONAL IN YOUR WORK

NAIL THE RECRUITING PROCESS

The word "intention" has become even more important to me after working with a tremendous coach who evaluates their team's ability to meet and set an intention each practice. When you win a game, you successfully execute the scouting plan. When you win a practice, you successfully execute the practice plan. When you win a workout, you successfully execute your workout plan. All of those plans are designed with intention.

Utilize the resources you have at your disposal to create an efficient and intentionally focused workout, designed for you to improve in the areas you are most limited in. Trim the stuff that doesn't matter.

If you get a chance, watch an individual workout at the highest levels of college basketball. Your mind will be blown by the simplicity. They rep the same things, over and over again, until a player can't get it wrong. This tends to frustrate younger college athletes, who want to grow faster than their body and minds tend to allow. As intolerable as frustration seems in the moment, navigating frustration is a skill that you will build as you do the work. Use these workouts as an intentional practice in developing patience with yourself.

YOU ARE FOCUSED ON FORM

Let's say you're working on quickening your release as a shooter. I've worked with shooters who tried to quicken their releases by catching the ball on a hop. Great. They would tell me they had it nailed down in their individual workouts. But then, once they started doing it in practices and games, they would travel on every catch because their footwork wasn't timed properly.

This detail should have been PERFECTED in their individual work. There's no point in working if you aren't doing it in a way that benefits you. Break down the small details of your form slowly. Get it right until you can't get it wrong. Then increase the speed.

YOU ARE AS MENTALLY AND PHYSICALLY ENGAGED AS YOU WOULD BE IN A PRACTICE

As a young athlete, one of the coolest things you can learn about is muscle memory. Muscle memory isn't just a phrase, it's a real thing. And the "memory" part is a result of the fatty acid called myelin enveloping a particular part of your nervous system with the skills you've practiced, and making them easier to repeat. This process, (referred to as myelination) has been extensively studied by the National Institute of Health, the Mayo Clinic, and legendary professor of Health Sciences, Dr. Ueli Suter.

To put it simply, the more reps you put in with the proper focus and intensity, the more that work will become hardwired in your body. What fires together, wires together. You can do it if you commit to it.

YOU ARE CONSISTENT

This one comes after the first three, because none of it matters unless you're consistent at both the micro and macro level.

MICRO: You are working as hard as you can (both physically and mentally) to get every detail right, on every rep. But that work only matters if you're doing it right every time. If that means you can only work for 20 minutes before the quality is compromised, then cut it at 20 minutes. Go hard and get it right.

MACRO: You schedule the days and times you work out and if you have to miss one, you make it up, promptly. The work only adds up to growth if you commit to doing it often and consistently. Log not only your workouts but how you did in them. Hold yourself accountable to trying to improve your performance in a drill the next time you try it. This will make for some great conversation points when you check back in with coaches.

Workout Misses

Below is a compilation of the biggest mistakes young people tend to make as they conduct a workout. You'd be wise to avoid them.

THE "INSTAGRAM OKIE DOKE"

People do stupid drills on social media to look cool. I'll admit that most of the time the drills look interesting, but don't help in any meaningful way. Take most of what you see on social media with a grain of salt because social media is not a real place. Put your blinders on and run your race.

YOU ARE DOING EVERYTHING, AND ALSO NOTHING

In my earlier coaching years, I was definitely guilty of facilitating workouts that accomplished nothing. Weirdly, the players loved them! Strange, right? Well, as I got older, I realized why. The players loved that we didn't lock in on one detail, so the energy was zipping the whole time.

But let's go a little further down that road.

If you do 10 different drills inside of a 25 minute workout, I can guarantee you three things:

1) You will be drenched in sweat
2) You will feel accomplished
3) You will not have gotten better at any of the skills you were working on

YOU ARE STATIONERY SHOOTING

Every sport has their version of stationery catch and shoot on the basketball court. I've heard tons of players proudly tell me they worked out on their own... what they actually did was plug in a shooting gun and catch and shoot the ball 500 times. Cool. That experience got them better at catching and shooting the ball, but it was with no defense and no movement at game speed. While not completely counter-productive, did it really help them improve at the thing they needed to? Like, if you just got beat on a backdoor-cut four times in one game, and you work to get better at this by shooting the ball 500 times, what problems have you solved?

Doing the plain work can be therapeutic for athletes, and I encourage them to continue doing it, but this work is not a substitute for the real growth-oriented work you need to do.

YOU ARE NOT HOLDING YOURSELF ACCOUNTABLE

When it comes to workouts, you need to be your own coach.

You need to honestly ask yourself "would a coach have accepted the effort I just gave?" If the answer is "no", you need to do it again. If you miss a time you scheduled, you need to hold yourself accountable like a coach would and make up for it.

Some of my favorite drills are "leave the gym" drills. In these drills, an athlete can't leave the gym until their goal is accomplished. Consider trying things like that to keep yourself locked in. Self-accountability is one of the ultimate skills that you can have as a prospective college athlete.

The Mac Line

I want to tell you about one of my former players to challenge any second thoughts you may have about putting in the work. We'll refer to her by her nickname, Mac.

Mac had a relentless motor. She tried out for the team as a first-year student and got her spot after finishing tied for first place in one of our team's conditioning tests. The scene was unforgettable. One of our captains was a determined competitor, and it was clear she was not going to lose to Mac. There was just one problem. Mac wouldn't stop running.

The two of them pushed each other so hard that the coaching staff agreed to call off the test after the pair ran an additional 15 more half-lengths of the court than anyone else on the team.

From a skill perspective, Mac was behind. From an attitude and work ethic perspective, Mac was top-tier. She was thrilled to be part of the team, and was our energy bus for four seasons, even as she spent a large part of her career dealing with injuries that kept her off the court once she had further developed her skills.

We found Mac's motor to be so inspiring that we actually built a team policy around it. Our coaching staff tracked every touch on a player (If we watched film with them, we tracked it, if we worked out with a player, we tracked it etc.) and we knew Mac was going to be the benchmark with at least two weekly touches. If you didn't meet Mac's benchmark, the coaching staff would not entertain a discussion with you about playing time. That benchmark was referred to as the "Mac Line."

EVERY COLLEGE COACH WANTS A MAC ON THEIR TEAM.

I posed a question to the CCQ based on a leadership seminar given by Simon Sinek. In his speech, he made a call for leaders to evaluate trustworthiness with the same urgency they would evaluate performance. With this call in mind, I asked the coaches to identify the lowest performance ability a player on their team could have if they knew that player would have a 10/10 attitude and be unconditionally trustworthy. I had them imagine a 10 as an All-American, and a 1 to be a non-athlete who was barely coordinated enough to be on the court or field.

Want to know something wild?

The average response (mean, median, AND mode) was a 5/10.

Even wilder?

The same number of scholarship level coaches and non-scholarship level coaches chose a 5/10.

How about TOTALLY UNHINGED?!

I was fortunate enough to collect data from more than 20 coaches who led their teams to one or more conference championships in their careers, and their average response was a 4.5/10.

Obviously, a successful college coach cannot fill their entire roster with 4.5/10 players. But when they have the ability to, you can bet your bottom dollar they're going to bring on a high motor recruit that has a great attitude.

College coaches value "glue" players who commit to the process and lift their teammates up with their attitude. If you build consistent growth habits in high school, you will also develop a winning attitude. And in your darkest and most doubtful moments, you need to remind yourself that all college coaches notice attitude.

Your goal is to improve in your growth areas. But even if you don't improve as much as you'd like, you will still build great habits in the process. I genuinely believe that most of the athletes I've interacted with as a college coach made it there because of habits they developed in high school.

FOR PARENTS/GUARDIANS:

I find sometimes that adults forget what separates them from kids. The biggest separator is that adults have survived their biggest mistakes, and children haven't made any big ones yet.

As a parent or guardian, you understand that your biggest mistakes fell into one of two categories:

1) A mistake that jeopardized a personal success
2) A mistake that jeopardized a personal relationship

Do not let your child make one of these mistakes because they are frustrated about the process.

It takes a tremendous amount of support and care to empathize with a child as they navigate the highs and lows of growth, so do your best to build up their confidence. When trouble arises, remind them of your confidence in their ability to solve the problem. Try to avoid solving the problem for them. Above all, don't let them quit. They can do this.

Help them track their progress in workouts. Aid them in developing reasonable goals. Where possible, collaborate with them or their mentors in facilitating workouts. It takes a village. They can do this. Believe in them.

SECTION 3

FINDING YOUR FIT

UNOFFICIAL CAMPUS VISITS

You've identified colleges and teams that could be ideal fits for you. It's time to embark on those campus visits with your family! To help frame the importance of each visit, I want to address one question for coaches that was intentionally omitted in the last section.

Where Do I Stand on Your Recruiting List for This Class?

Knowing where you stand on a coaching staff's recruiting list will often be a key motivator for deciding to visit in the first place. Coaches realize that. So, it certainly makes sense why you'd want to know that information.

But there is something else you should know about your standing.

Your visit is not just your opportunity to gauge a coaching staff. It goes both ways. It's also their time to gauge you. And there is some really interesting data about how much your rank can change based on how your visits go.

First, you need to remember that coaches are often "old-school" personality types who value direct and in-person communication. The CCQ strongly agreed that they prefer, whenever possible, to offer roster spots to recruits in person. That answer did not change for any sport, or any competitive level. Coaches will use their quality time with you on a visit to determine if you are a fit for their program.

Much like every part of this process, there are exceptions that could lead a coach to offer a roster spot in advance of a visit. The CCQ highlighted three examples.

1) You're a prospect who would have to travel extensively to visit the campus. A coach may strategically offer you a spot in advance to incentivize such considerable travel.
2) It's very late in the process (at the earliest, your senior year of high school), so an offer becomes a tool for a team to get on your radar in an expedited fashion.
3) You are a top national recruit that has already been flooded with roster spot offers, so a coaching staff offers you in early conversations just so you know they're serious about pursuing you.

If you ask where you stand before your first visit to a campus, you may not get a definitive response. A coach may say you're at or near the top of their list, or that they have several recruits ahead of you at your position, or you might get the middle ground and learn that you're in their mix but that it's still early in their process. Regardless of what you hear, you should not be discouraged if you don't get an offer. It just means you're experiencing the most common recruiting path.

Does That Mean My Behavior is Being Evaluated by the Coaching Staff While I'm on My Visit?

Yes, it does. Remember earlier in the book when I told you that coaches were watching you closely? That's not just happening at your games. Your behavior and body language on visits is being watched, too.

Two of the most extreme CCQ responses were about visits. I asked them if a prospect could move from a "maybe" to a "yes" if they were engaged and showcased a positive attitude on their campus visit. The median response was a 9, and the most common a 10. Sustain eye contact, ask good questions, be present in your experience, and you can *FLY* up a staff's list.

I then flipped the question to a negative, and asked about how a disengaged or negative campus visitor might change their standing as a result. Could this move a recruit from a "yes" to a "maybe," or even a "no"? The responses were nearly identical, with the median being a 9 and most common a 10. So go right ahead and spend your visit being a dud and staring at your phone, just don't act surprised when you wind up falling down the list.

As we dive into our discussion on unofficial visits, it is crucial that you remember the importance of the engagement and awareness components of your GEAR.

But What if I'm introverted?

Good! Introverts play crucial roles on both teams and coaching staffs. They are generally more observant, great listeners, and have outstanding critical thinking skills. You can display all of those qualities on a visit. Coaches don't need to hear you dominate a conversation to know you are engaged. Your positive, engaged energy can translate through good posture, body language, and eye contact. If the presence of your voice is normally a 5/10, then be a 5/10. Just showcase the other things that make you the standout candidate you are.

Now, onto the main topic of the chapter!

Unofficial Visits

An unofficial visit (UV) tends to be the first campus visit involving a coaching staff. It is also one that the college cannot subsidize in any way, regardless of competitive level. That means coaching staffs cannot pay or reimburse you for any travel expenses or food that you eat while you are there.

A typical UV features a tour of the campus and athletic facilities, as well as a chat with coaches. Depending on how far your relationship has progressed with a staff before your UV, the visit may also include watching a practice or game, spending time with some current members of the team, doing a film breakdown with coaches, meeting a professor or department chair in your academic area of interest, and (current trend alert) doing a photoshoot where you can picture yourself in that team's uniform.

The organization of a UV will provide some contextual clues about where you stand on a coach's big board. If a coaching staff considers you a high recruiting priority, they will likely initiate a conversation with you to schedule a campus visit. A member of their staff will then likely build out an itinerary for you and lead your campus tour.

If they don't do this, don't panic! This does not mean you are not an option for a school, those are just clues that a coaching staff is interested. That said, you should aim to follow the heat the same way coaches do. If you can tell a coaching staff is interested in you and wants you to visit, you should prioritize that visit.

There isn't necessarily a right or wrong time of year to do an unofficial visit, and ultimately both parties need to accommodate each other's schedules. Just know that if you do an unofficial visit during a time that classes are not in session, you will not get a truly vibrant campus experience and it will be hard to accurately assess that college. Be strategic with that piece of information. I'm not saying don't do it while school is out, but if you do choose to do your UV outside the academic year, schedule another visit during it. You can also make sure your official visit takes place during a time you can experience a functioning day of the campus (for example a Friday into Saturday, or a Sunday into Monday).

What Coaches Want Out of the UV

A coaching staff wants to accomplish two things with your visit. First, they want to sell their program and their campus to you. Second, they want to make sure you are in alignment with them and will be a solid addition to their team. They'll ask you questions regarding your values and interests in order to ascertain if their school and staff are a match. They also want to specifically gauge your interest in developing as an athlete, so you should expect them to ask you sport related questions. They may also ask questions of your family, as this is likely the first time they will meet in person.

The UV will include a lot of information being thrown at you at once. But the intent behind the information overload is good. A staff wants to know if you are interested in what they're selling.

What You Need to Get Out of the UV

As a recruit, you need to be confident about the following five areas by the end of a UV:

1) *You have a gut feeling that you could be both academically and athletically successful there.*

A coaching staff's network on campus is a huge sign of their holistic investment in you. You should feel like your questions about both academic and athletic success have been satisfactorily answered. You should also have been networked with resources on campus and shown the specific paths to success.

NAIL THE RECRUITING PROCESS

2) You know you will be supported by the staff if you attend that school.

You should know concretely that there are people like you currently enrolled at their school, and that those people are flourishing on and off the court or field. Look out for coaching staffs that specifically highlight physical and mental wellness, as well as balance.

Get a feel of what the coaches are like "behind the scenes" and what structures are in place to keep players from falling through the cracks.

3) You feel an attraction to the people, not the sales pitch.

There is a component to the working world that you may not understand as a young person, and I'm going to do my best to explain it to you now. Even if you LOVE your job, you will still hate around 10-15% of your actual job responsibilities.

Even though coaches love the recruiting process for a multitude of reasons, they hate photo shoots, swag giveaways, and other promotions that they're forced to do to appeal to young people. There is no coach on the planet who actually enjoys custom making you a graphic in photoshop after spending eight to ten hours working with their current team earlier that day!

Coaching staffs do these things to make you feel like you're special to them, but they have to hype themselves up to actually do them. You don't have to get hyped up though. I promise you that by the time you are a college athlete, the photoshoots and swag that you posted on Instagram and TikTok will not matter to you at all. So, I'm going to encourage you to try not to let it matter now. A quality photoshoot or a brand-new arena is not greater than, or even equal to, the quality of the people hosting your visit. Do not let the shiny things distract you.

Similarly, and especially on a UV, trust that you are exclusively seeing the best of what that campus has to offer. College admissions offices literally design tour routes to highlight the great stuff and hide the bad stuff on their campuses. It's a sales pitch, after all! If you notice something is omitted from your visit, you need to ask about it. You can learn a lot about a staff by how they answer your questions about what is missing from the tour.

Several athletes shared with me that they actually built trust with their coaches because they were willing to share with them some of their perceived limitations of the campus or team. Even though the recruits were learning about a weakness, they were hearing something honest, and this honestly was not present in all of their visits.

4) You have a sense of how you will be used in their system of play.

If a staff doesn't deliberately show you film or do a chalk talk session with you on your visit, you should be asking them to describe their style of play in detail. Once you know their style of play, you should ask them how you fit into it. You can heighten your comfort with this information by watching a practice or game. Ask coaches if there is a certain player on the current roster who matches your skill set, then keep an eye on what they're working on when you watch them play.

5) You know where you stand on their recruiting list by the end of your visit.

Remember the big question from earlier in the chapter? If you haven't done so already, this is when you ask it. If your visit went well, and the coaching staff thinks that you are both a talent and attitude fit, there is a chance you get offered a roster spot right there and then.

If you are not offered a roster spot, a coach should let you know where you stand. For example, if there is someone ahead of you at your position, or you're in the mix with a few other players, a coach will usually tell you as much.

I understand how discouraging it can be in the moment to know that coaches may want someone else more than you. Please remember in these moments how imperfect the science of recruiting is. Coaches tend to aim for the moon, and thus, their boards tend to fluctuate like the tides throughout the academic year. Until a coach definitively says no to you, stay engaged and keep in strong communication with them.

Handling Offers

If you are offered a roster spot…

LET'S GOOOOOOOOOOOOO!!!!!!!!!

You and your family should be thrilled! You were just told the thing you've been dreaming about is going to come to fruition. That's amazing!

A coach has made it clear to you that you are a priority recruit for them, so this is the time when you and your parents should ask a few key questions about what the offer entails.

There may not be a ton of questions if you are offered a full athletic scholarship that also covers the cost of attendance. But if you get an offer at the non-scholarship level, it will be critical for your family to get further information about financial aid, net price calculators, merit money, and other avenues for seeking tuition assistance. If opportunities for NIL money are important to you, this is also another appropriate time to ask about that.

A head coach may also use this time to ask you where their program stands on your list. Be as honest with them as you can in your response. If you loved the experience but know there are a few other places you also love, it's fair to say that you're very interested and they're in your top tier. If your dream school just offered you a spot, let them know they are your top choice.

From there, you'll usually learn about a timeline for a potential commitment. Most coaches are not expecting you to commit immediately. In fact, when I asked the CCQ if they expected immediate responses to a roster spot offer, the average response was a 2.

NAIL THE RECRUITING PROCESS

But you won't have an indefinite amount of time to decide either. Coaches don't want to lose you, and they also don't want to lose the recruits behind you on their board while you take your sweet time to decide. They will usually point you towards specific dates that they will need a decision by.

In certain circumstances, when the iron is really hot with a school, they may have more offers out than spots available. This could require you to make a quicker decision than you want to. If this happens, schedule an official visit promptly, and get in touch with your mentors to start breaking down every part of your experience with this school.

If a coach pushes you to make an immediate decision, it may forecast future problems with that coach. A rushed decision is usually one made based on fear rather than certainty. If a coach is compelling you to make fear-based decisions before you're even a college student, that coach is probably not done using fear as a motivator. Fear-based motivation tactics can destroy relationships between coaches and players.

You likely will not experience the above scenario on your unofficial visit, but if you do, consider it a red flag. Otherwise, this is a really exciting moment that will help you further narrow down your choices!

#NotCommitted

A common trend in modern recruiting is for recruits to post on social media when they receive an offer after a visit or productive phone call. My opinion on this behavior has changed, largely because of the interviews I conducted with coaches for this book.

Initially, I advised against the practice of posting offers because I found some of the posts to be overly self-indulgent and distasteful. But in the modern age of recruiting, coaches are monitoring social media. If you post about an offer you received, it may actually light a fire under some staffs to begin the recruiting process with you. It is very annoying that some coaches use this kind of thing to inform their recruiting decisions, but it definitely is a reality… so post away!

But don't go overboard. If you post that you received an offer, keep it short and sweet. Thank the head coach and other staff members involved for their time and consideration, and express gratitude that they offered you a roster spot. Be tasteful. Let's take a moment to walk through the stupidity of the recent "#NotCommitted" trend. Imagine if you thought you just had a great visit with a specific school, then open up Instagram to see the head coach on that staff post the following:

"Had a top recruit on campus. They were cool, but I don't really know if we're interested."

That would make you feel pretty crappy, right? Coaches put a lot of time into making sure you have a good visit. Why would you reply with a message that suggests you aren't sure that you're interested in them, let alone do it in the very message that thanks them for having you? Your recruiting experience is not a reality show. Don't try to turn it into one.

The Big Board

There is no such thing as too many unofficial visits. If you need to visit a specific campus more than once, do it. If you need to do 20 visits to 20 different campuses in order to figure out what you want, do it. There is no right way to handle this process.

Once you feel like you have the information you need, it's time to hit the big board.

The same way that coaches rank their recruits is the way you now need to rank your choices. Stack the components of your visits up against one another. Assess which places have the most of what you want. Feeling stuck and looking for tiebreakers? Here are some elements to consider:

a) Where do you currently have offers?
b) Where can you get in?
c) Where did you get the gut feeling that you could be academically and athletically successful?
d) Which schools have your favorite academic programs?
e) Which schools have your favorite coaching staffs?
f) Which schools are financially viable for you and your family?
g) What concerns did you have about each of your visits?

After enough time sifting through this information with your mentors and your family, you should have narrowed down your list to a few schools. These are the schools you should schedule official visits with.

While there is no longer a limit to the number of official visits you can go on, they are time consuming and can be overwhelming. Aim for between two and five schools. In my opinion, five is actually too many. That said, I have interacted with less decisive people who really needed the variety to inform their decision. Two is the absolute minimum, for reasons we will discuss next chapter.

As a quick aside, I do know some recruits who were so confident they found the right fit that they decided to commit after their UV. Their later visits were mostly done to meet more people and gather more information. This ended up being the right decision for them, but you should feel no pressure at all if this isn't your approach.

The Breakup Call

In good standing with a lot of places? Well, congrats! Now you may have to make some calls and break the hearts of some head coaches. Just kidding, they're used to it. Just respectfully tell them you're going to go in a different direction. And I said tell them… like with your voice. I didn't say email them or text them. GEAR up and call them on the phone. You may need to text them to set up a time to talk, but that's it.

Coaches hear "no" way more than they hear "yes" on the recruiting trail. Trust that this is part of the process, and that coaches know how to handle it. On the off chance they handle it poorly, congrats on being validated in your choice to not proceed further with that coach.

It's not fun to be turned down, but coaches get it, and you can be tactful in the conversation. Here is a basic script you can stick to.

"I really want to thank you and your staff for taking the time to recruit me. I've enjoyed getting to know more about your staff and your program, but at this time, I am going to explore options that I think are a better fit for me. If anything changes, I will reach back out Thank you again for your continued interest and support, and I wish you the best of luck moving forward with your recruiting process."

This may be the first time you've ever had to do something like this, but it's important to do, not only for the sake of your continued growth, but also for the sake of keeping options open. Why? Because things can happen with admissions or with coaching staffs after you make a commitment, so do not burn bridges, especially with coaching staffs that you liked. You never know where both you and they may end up.

FOR PARENTS/GUARDIANS:

Your role in this part of your child's journey is like that of a guide, in the passenger seat while on a road trip. The driver knows the eventual destination, but may not know exactly how to get there, and you have the map. Your kid won't get this analogy. We remember the days before GPS. They weren't there. Oof!

You know what sales pitches look like, and therefore have the ability to spot authenticity faster than a teenager. Use those skills to guide the driver from the passenger seat. If you have questions for coaching staffs or things about your child that you want to share, campus visits are the perfect opportunity to discuss those items.

While staffs are in sales mode on these visits, remember that they are also assessing you and that the line is fine between a family member who is adding value to a conversation and a family member who is dominating it and speaking for their child. There is also a behavioral cue that you need to be aware of. Nearly half of the CCQ described a strategy they use on visits when they feel like a recruit's parents are monopolizing the conversation. Look out for this behavior in yourself, and know to return to the passenger seat if you see yourself doing it.

If you finish saying something during a meeting with the staff and a coach responds by specifically asking a question directly at your child, it's an indicator that you've been talking too much. Internalize that cue, and respect it.

Your family will probably be experiencing information overload by the time you hit the end of a visit. The drive home is where you and your child get to process that information. It's also a great venue for you to express any concerns that you may have had during the visit and hear how your child feels about them.

NAIL THE RECRUITING PROCESS

Take some time to debrief with your child before you hit the big board. Even if they say it doesn't matter, your opinion really does matter to your child. They're listening more than you think they are. Be a great navigator, just do it while staying in that passenger seat!

OFFICIAL CAMPUS VISITS

You've worked your tail off to grow as an athlete and get recruited, and now you're in the home stretch. It's often the most exciting, but also the most unnerving time. You know big decisions are just around the corner. The last step before you make that decision tends to be going on official visits.

An Official visit (OV) is usually reserved for the top recruits in each class that have either already received roster spot offers, or will be receiving one if the visit goes well. On official campus visits, schools are allowed to fund your meals, activities, and (depending on competitive level and institutional policy) your lodging and travel expenses. These visits will also provide you quality time with your potential future teammates. At higher competitive levels, your family will be a part of many of your OV experiences as well.

In essence, this is the final fit test for both sides.

What Coaches Want Out of the OV

For coaches, an official visit is simultaneously the biggest sell and the biggest investigation. Coaching staffs will engage in more conversations with both you and your family. There will be specific meeting times built into your itinerary to make you feel as secure as possible with them.

When it comes to your time away from the coaches, you will traditionally be paired with a "host," who is a current member of the team. Recruits usually stay overnight in the host's room. Additionally, the host and their teammates will usually participate in some activities with you. These activities will usually be built around your interests.

Your host is there to show you a good time. They were also picked to host you intentionally. Hosts are players the coaching staff unconditionally trust as ambassadors for their team. You also need to know that the coaching staff will be talking extensively to your host about how the visit went afterwards.

In my personal experience, I can tell you that three of my personal favorite recruits did not end up on my teams because of negative feedback they received from their hosts. In all three of these instances, the host was acting as a protector of the team's culture, and expressed concerns (backed by the rest of their teammates) about inappropriate behaviors that the recruit either talked about or engaged in while on the visit. These behaviors included a recruit repeatedly asking their hosts to break away from the itinerary and take them to a party on a school night, conversations in which a recruit disparaged their current and former teammates and coaches, and even one instance when a recruit left the team to hang out with other local friends, and did not return texts and phone calls when the team couldn't find them.

NAIL THE RECRUITING PROCESS

The highest average CCQ response in all of my questioning for this book was about whether a CCQ solicited feedback from their current players at the end of a visit. The average response (and remember, this is for 50 coaches) was a 9.4.

If you have been consistently developing your GEAR, then you should have nothing to worry about on this visit... besides the typical nerves that arise when you'll be engaging with a bunch of new people for the first time! But on these official visits you still need to be hyper-aware of your language and behavior. Especially if you are visiting a team with a good reputation, the current players tend to be very protective of their program.

What You Need to Get Out of the OV

That awareness works both ways, and the official visit is the forum for you to address your deepest concerns with a coaching staff. Your question bank should be fully exhausted by the end of an OV.

We will be learning best practices for OVs exclusively from the players I spoke to. They used their official visits to gauge three specific components of a team and staff. We will refer to them as the three C's.

Care

The players were able to identify coaches who authentically cared about them as people, both on and off the court or field. One player expressed a deliberate decision to work with a coach they felt was less experienced but more caring, and went on to say that the visible level of care drove the team culture. Another asked coaches what they do to celebrate and value their players as people, and felt they could tell which coaches were more invested from the content of their responses.

One player I spoke to had a family member with a terminal illness, and asked coaches how they would handle the situation as it got heavier. By asking deliberate questions about this, the player was able to identify the coaching staff they felt were best equipped to support them from both their body language and their words. Here was their comment:

"You never know where a conversation is going to lead. Let it go there and see what happens. This allows you to put emphasis on the off-court relationships."

Comfort

On the court or field, there is no growth in the comfort zone. But off of it, your environment does need to provide you comfort in order for you to be able to grow optimally. Players interviewed used their visits to assess their comfort level not only with the staff and team, but with the greater campus community. They wanted to feel comfortable and welcomed as their authentic selves on the campus they were visiting.

A specific strategy to gauge comfort came up multiple times in my interviews. During team time away from coaches, the players identified a current team member that they deemed trustworthy and asked them much deeper and more intentional questions about their experience. These questions tended to be more about safety and security, and less about sport performance. Recruits asked about mental health, coaches' behavior behind the scenes, and the actual closeness and chemistry of the team.

When it comes to comfort, you have to feel it in your gut. Your instincts will tell you whether or not you can flourish in a specific environment if you ask enough questions. There might be such a thing as asking too many questions to gauge comfort on a visit, but I certainly haven't seen it happen yet. Coaches and players alike want to know you're invested in being a contributing member of their team. If you ask good questions, you can trust that you will be judged as someone trying to find the right place for themselves, and nothing more.

Consistency

The "Say/Do Matrix" is a graph used by many prominent leadership consultants. The Y axis is the "say," or how well a leader delivers a message on a scale of 1 to 10, and the X axis is the "do," or how well a leader actually lives the message they discussed.

Coaches say the right thing. But coaches are also often people with stubborn personality types. Because of this, some coaches struggle to live what they say.

Below are some "Say/Do Matrix" inconsistencies that came up in my interviews with athletes. There were some notable inconsistencies shared by players who ended up having great four-year experiences. Unfortunately, the more glaring inconsistencies came from players who transferred. Of note, none of them involved playing time.

a) A coach said they wanted to press or play up-tempo (basketball lingo for exciting and fast), and then either couldn't manage an up-tempo team or didn't ever try an up-tempo style of play.
b) A coach said that a specific recruit was an ideal fit for their system or said that a part of the system would change to accommodate that recruit's skill set, and neither thing happened.
c) A coach said that they valued transparency and welcomed "tough" conversations, but then struggled to have direct conversations with players about their positions on the depth chart.
d) A coach said their number one priority was team culture, but the team was visibly "cliquey" and disjointed. An additional culture related example is that of a coach who was unwilling to have conversations with key players that were clearly hurting the team culture.
e) A coach adamantly informed a recruit that they planned to stay in their position long term, beyond the length of their current coaching contract. That coach then left to take a new job before their initial contract had even expired.
f) A coach spoke passionately about player development, but then did not make themselves available for the extra film sessions or player workouts that would make that a reality.

NAIL THE RECRUITING PROCESS

I found players sharing these examples to be so powerful that if I choose to write another book, it would be a book targeted at college coaches about these glitches in the "Say/Do Matrix."

The coaching community is filled with aspiringly good people; the kind of people that constantly seek out knowledge about self and team improvement. But that doesn't mean they're actually proficient at those skills! And it certainly doesn't mean they deploy those skills consistently. A good but inconsistent person can still frustrate the ever-loving crap out of you! And a situation where you feel misled by an inconsistent coach can lead to resentment, anxiety, and even broken relationships...

SO, YOU HAVE TO FILTER FOR THIS STUFF ON YOUR OFFICIAL VISIT.

Here's the plan. Remember the previous blurb about finding a trustworthy person and asking them the important questions about the realities of a program and campus? Use that same person (or people) to gauge for consistency. Share some of the questions that you asked the coaches, as well as how those coaches responded. Then ask the players, point blank, "How true is this?"

It won't seem like the most important part of your visit in that moment, but I promise that future-you will thank present-you for doing it. Ask the tough and uncomfortable questions and then listen not only for the content and tone of the responses, but also for the things that are not said. Often the things missing from a response can be what lead your gut one way or another.

I Had a Great Visit, Do I Need to Commit?

There are a bunch of different scenarios that may make you to want to commit on the spot, and they largely depend on the timing of your visit. It's much easier to explain the wrong time to commit. If you feel pressured to commit on the spot, or if you are pressuring yourself internally to make a decision that doesn't sit right with your gut, don't commit.

Remember, coaches overwhelmingly are not expecting commitments on the spot, and will instead communicate a timeline to you. If you feel so good about how a visit went that you are prepared to say "bump your timeline, this is my place, I'm all in," then by all means go for it! In any other situation, adhere to the process of elimination in your visits.

I have found that recruits tend to find one singular campus and team that they consider to be a perfect match for them. I refer to that visit as the "bar setting" visit. The tricky part here is how that visit could be your very first visit, and could also be your last visit. You only really know which visit sets the bar by experiencing the other visits that don't resonate with your gut as much to serve as a comparison. This is the reason you should do a minimum of two OVs. If you go on two visits, you will definitely have a better experience on one of them. If you go on a third or fourth, then you can rank the visits and really establish where the bar is. The school that becomes the bar is the best fit.

One of the players I spoke to utilized an awesome approach to find their bar. They felt in their gut that the first school they had an OV with was ultimately going to be the best place for them. Here is what they said to the head coach.

"I just want to let you know that I really think your program and your school are the right place for me. But I also feel like I owe it to myself and my family to go on the other visit I already scheduled, so I can compare my experiences and confirm that your school is the right fit."

There is no possible way that you, a kid, can say something similar to them, an adult, and be greeted with anything except for respect. If you are, cross that coach off your list. They don't get it!

From here, you nail your choice in three simple steps.

1) You continue your scheduled visits until you have the bar set.
2) You revisit your big board and talk extensively with your family and mentors to confirm that the bar is right.
3) You commit (more on this next chapter).

I'm Not Getting Offers to Come on Official Visits to My Favorite Schools... What Do I Do?

The major official visit season tends to be in the fall of your senior year of high school. It can be very challenging to feel your dream is in jeopardy because you aren't invited on any official visits at that time. If you're feeling this way as you read along, you need to remember three important things.

1) This process is different for everybody.
2) You can keep engaging with coaches and exploring options, and your mentors can help you do this.
3) You've been building your GEAR for a reason.

Keep networking with coaches. Keep producing new film. Keep getting feedback from your mentors. KEEP DOING IT ALL. You've come this far. Don't give up now. In my time working in college sports, we have signed athletes as late as June of their senior year of high school, only weeks before they graduated.

Even then, you can still try out for a team and walk on. Remember, your GEAR will set you apart. So, stay up. Trust in your own process.

One last thing to consider before you decide to commit.

You may not recognize the name "John Wooden," but you can expect every coach in your orbit to know about him. Why? Because every coach that emphasizes personal development through sports has Wooden's face on their coaching Mt. Rushmore. In addition to being an outstanding basketball coach, Wooden pioneered the "Pyramid of Success," a model outlining the developmental journey needed to achieve competitive greatness.

Wooden's illustrious career with UCLA men's basketball included a decade of dominance that will likely never be matched, in any sport. From 1963 to 1973, the UCLA men's basketball program went an astonishing 281-15, winning nine out of a possible ten NCAA National Championships.

Coach Wooden mentored several of the greatest men's basketball players to ever grace the court. I want to focus on one of them. In the tail end of his career, Wooden was searching for a center to replace the legendary Kareem Abdul-Jabbar (known then as Lew Alcindor). His #1 target was a near seven-footer with a free spirit from La Mesa, California. His name was Bill Walton. You may recognize the name. After all, Walton is enshrined in the basketball hall of fame alongside Abdul-Jabbar and Wooden. But I want you to learn more about Bill Walton, the recruit. In a recent speaking engagement, Walton shared memories of the hundreds of sales pitches he received from college coaches. They promised him championships, accolades, jobs… and in some cases, even dates with cheerleaders! Coach Wooden took a different approach. Here is Walton's account of Coach Wooden's first recruiting visit.

"My life was irrevocably changed when John Wooden walked into our family home… the same family home that my mom still lives in… He looks at my mom and my dad, looks at me and he says 'Billy and Mr. and Mrs. Walton, I know what all the other schools are promising you. That's not the way life works. There's no guarantees out there. The only thing I can promise you is I'll give you a chance – a chance to be a part of something special. But being a part of something special, that's a privilege Billy, and you gotta earn it every single day.' And then he turned to me and he said 'If you want to be the champion in everything that you do, you have to understand that it's not how good you are Billy, it's how good your teammates are... Your ultimate level of achievement, accomplishment, happiness, and success is not going to be based on just you.'"

Bill Walton was sold. He enrolled at UCLA, where he won two national championships and was named national player of the year in all three of his active seasons.

The only promise that the most successful coach in the history of his sport made to the best recruit in the nation was that he was going to give him an opportunity to grow as a person every day. That initial pitch was made to Bill Walton more than 50 years ago, and it still makes me want to run through a brick wall for Coach Wooden.

COMMIT TO YOUR COACH WOODEN.

Commit to the coach who you know will challenge you to grow and who you trust will support you every step of the way. In your recruiting journey, you are going to encounter many different coaches who have many different recruiting tactics. As you get closer to making your final decision, I implore you to choose the staff and environment that promises you growth and not stuff. If the promise of your GEAR being refined every day is good enough for the all-time greats, it will be good enough for you too.

FOR PARENTS/GUARDIANS:

If you've been following the instructions provided here, you have likely exercised a lot of restraint when it comes to your correspondence with the other adults involved in this process.

NAIL THE RECRUITING PROCESS

Good news. You can hulk out now!

I want you to compare an official visit to that part of the car buying experience right after you just test drove your favorite car. You know you want it, but you need some more information about the deal. Meanwhile, the dealer can smell the potential sale and is going to do everything they can to try and reel you in to buy it. In this situation, you know what you'd do. You wouldn't settle for a car that didn't have all the features you wanted and all the safety and peace of mind needed to feel good about it.

Your child will be experiencing the visit in a different way, and filtering for their fit. You need to experience the visit as pragmatically as you possibly can. If a coach asks you what more you need to know, answer honestly. Let that conversation go in whatever direction it may lead.

Drive the car however you need to in your test drive to ensure that you feel safe letting your child drive that car off into their future.

The older you get, the less impulsive your decisions tend to be. Don't let your child rush into this. Debrief, debrief, and debrief some more. If you still feel unsure about the best path forward, this is the right time to have a follow up conversation with the child's mentors or the college coach in question. You have done an amazing job letting your child lead discussions to this point. Now is when you can take the lead and cover your child's blind spots.

If, after all your filtering, you still feel like you need more guidance, I'm always here! Reach out to me any time at RecruitingGEAR@gmail.com or @JaredTheCoach on most social media platforms that you'd expect someone in their late 30s to be using. I'm happy to help.

This will be my last message directly to you as parents in this book, so thank you so much for your time and consideration, and I hope you found this information helpful.

COMMITTING AND BEYOND

You've revisited your big board, you've debriefed extensively with your parents, and you have now found your fit. Congratulations friendo! You're ready to commit.

Step 1: The Commitment

Shoot your future head coach a text message that says something like, "Hey coach, I have some good news I'd like to share. Can we set up a time to talk?" You can omit the first part, but just know that you'll be giving your future head coach a panic attack because they'll assume you're calling to turn them down.

Let them know you would like to commit to being a part of their program, and tell them why. After some awesome moments of mutual gratitude and excitement, they will walk you through the next steps. Depending on the competitive level you're at, this will include some combination of athletics related paperwork, admissions related paperwork, and basic financial aid and demographic paperwork. Coaches are very familiar with the matriculating and onboarding process, and they will guide you from that point forward.

As your conversation with your future head coach comes to a close, request 72 hours of grace before your decision is made public. This will give you time to tie up your loose ends and end your other recruiting relationships tactfully - that last part is important, remember?

Step 2: Breathe

YOU DID IT! You dreamed of this day, and it has arrived. Celebrate with your family, thank your mentors, cherish this moment with the people who helped guide you. This is the beginning of your next chapter.

Step 3: Call the coaches from the other schools you visited

Don't text, don't email, and definitely don't "ghost them." CALL THEM. Let them know that you enjoyed your recruiting process with them but you ultimately found a better fit for yourself elsewhere. If you had a strong relationship with a head coach, they may ask you a few questions for the sake of assessment. I would encourage you to answer them honestly. Ultimately, any coach worth their salt will respect your gut decision to attend the school that best fits you.

It's important to take these steps, because you never 100% know what happens next. I obviously hope that by following the steps laid out in this book you found the perfect fit and will have a smooth college experience from here on out. But on the off chance you didn't find that fit or it falls through, you taking this step keeps your relationships with other coaches in good standing.

Step 4: DON'T PUT DOWN YOUR GEAR

By now, you have probably figured out the real strategy behind this book. This book is designed to teach you what college coaches expect from their current athletes. By utilizing those hard and soft skills as a high school athlete, you will SHINE in the recruiting process, because you are ahead of the game.

So, you better not put that GEAR away now.

My final question to the CCQ was open ended. I asked them to address any topic of their choosing. More than 10% of them made a point of saying in some way that your recruiting process is not over until the day you arrive on campus for your first day of school. Do not make academic, athletic, or personal decisions that would jeopardize your standing with your future team.

As long as you continue to grow, engage, and stay aware, you will be ready for the journey ahead.

Thank you!!!

As you complete this book, I hope you feel excited about what you've learned, and even more excited about putting it into practice. You dug way deeper than the average high school student does for this process, and you should be very proud of yourself.

If you feel like you still need guidance of any kind, or just want to say hello, please feel free to reach out to me. I would LOVE to hear how your process is going, and if this book helped you achieve your dream, I want to celebrate you! My social media handle is always @JaredTheCoach and you can also email me anytime at RecruitingGEAR@gmail.com. Like most coaches, my cell phone is attached to me any time I'm not asleep or in a practice/game. I will respond as quickly as I can.

Finally, I have one small story to share, just to motivate you and keep you pulling through your biggest moments of doubt.

Right before I started doing my research for this book, I received news from my doctors that my return to full-time work would again be delayed by a minimum of six months. In my current condition, I can exert myself (both mentally and physically) for around two to three hours a day before I have to rest for the remainder of the day. At times, this has felt like a mental and physical prison. But thanks to the advice of key friends and mentors, I was able to keep my eyes on the prize of small but sustained growth.

Every part of this book (from the research, to the interviews, to drafts, to editing, to marketing and publishing) was achieved in 45-minute daily increments. That is not a misprint. I spent 45 minutes a day on this book, for six months, and I feel more accomplished having completed it than I did from winning any basketball game or running any endurance race that I thought defined me and my identity.

I promise you that if you put 45 minutes a day into your GEAR, you are going to travel further than you can possibly imagine.

It will not only set you up for success, but will also change the way you think about learning and growing.

YOU CAN DO THIS.

Once you do, please reach out to me so we can celebrate together.

Finally, if you have found this book helpful, please leave a review on the website you purchased it from. Reviews will not only let me know of your experiences; they also help guide future readers like you.

I welcome any feedback you may have. Please take a few moments and leave it:

NailTheRecruitingProcess.com/review

Thank you for your time. Now go get it. It's yours for the taking.

Sincerely,
Jared

CCQ QUESTIONNAIRE DATA

Introduction

Thanks for reading the fun stuff. If you're interested, here comes the dorky stuff (WOO HOO!!!).

For the overall design of this book, my data gathering process consisted of three parts:

1) Fifty college coaches completed a questionnaire either by phone or on a dedicated survey page. Coaches identified themselves to me for demographic and sorting purposes only. This became the raw CCQ data, which will be shared in this section.
2) I spoke to 15 of those 50 coaches, as well as many of my former colleagues and mentors to gauge their reactions to the data. These interviews added important layers of context to the rationale of coaches in the recruiting process.
3) I interviewed 10 current or former college athletes to get their input on both their recruiting processes and the CCQ data.

JARED ZEIDMAN

I elected to keep the identities of the participants anonymous. They were clearly willing to share more once they knew they would not be identified in the final publication. The interviews informed most of the qualitative information in the book, so it would be redundant to share additional interview findings here. The CCQ data, however, was the engine that drove the book, so it is important to me that you get to see it.

This is certainly not meant to be a dissertation, but I still want to express two limitations before I share the data itself. First, there was no part of this process that was "blind." All of the participants knew, at an absolute minimum, my identity and my intentions with the data. I do not believe this is a significant issue, since this book was not written with the intention of academic publication, but being transparent about it is important to me.

Second, 50 coaches are not 500 coaches, so the total number of responses certainly suggests the need for greater research on this subject. That said, the CCQ had very strong and uniform responses to almost all of the questions. I draw additional attention to this in the presentation of the data wherever applicable by using a sub-category titled "response clustering." Because of the presence of these response clusters, I have reason to believe that even if we quadrupled the response pool, we would have very similar responses. This data solidifies my opinion that coaches are an extremely like-minded group of individuals who happen to have different personality and stylistic traits that differentiate them.

Research Methods:

Participants were asked to respond to 17 prompts on a scale of 1-10. The prompts were divided into three sections and the prompt meanings were outlined at the beginning of each section. Participants also responded to four open-ended questions. If a participant elected to be interviewed by phone, they were given an opportunity to provide a rationale for their responses. These explanations were transcribed.

Demographics:

- 62% Female Respondents*
- 38% Male Respondents*
- 48% Athletic Scholarship Level Coaches
- 52% Non-Athletic-Scholarship Level Coaches
- 15% Control Group of non-basketball coaches**

Upon sorting average responses by gender identity, I discovered no discernable difference in responses. There was no question where the average response between an identified male and female coach differed by a full point (the highest, was .9, and it only occurred once). Therefore, I do not sort any of the responses by gender identity.

** Response clusters were so consistent across demographics that I wanted to control for responses from coaches of other sports.

Section 1: Basic Recruit Background Questions
(1 = Completely Disagree, 10 = Completely Agree)

1) **A top-tier recruit needs to be on a reputable AAU or Club team.**
   Mean Response: 4.25
   Median Response: 3
   Most Common Response: 3
   Scholarship level mean response: 4.75
   Non-scholarship level mean response: 3.75
   Control Group mean: 3.5
   Response clustering (if applicable): n/a

2) **A top-tier recruit needs to be on a reputable High School team.**
   Mean Response: 3.28
   Median Response: 3
   Most Common Response: 1
   Scholarship level mean response: 3.8
   Non-scholarship level mean response: 2.75
   Control Group mean: 1.25
   Response clustering (if applicable): 80% of total responses were a 5 or lower

3) **A top-tier recruit needs to be a single sport athlete.**
   Mean Response: 1.5
   Median Response: 1
   Most Common Response: 1
   Scholarship level mean response: 1.5
   Non-scholarship level mean response: 1.5

NAIL THE RECRUITING PROCESS

Control Group mean: 1
Response clustering (if applicable): 49 of 50 responses were a 4 or lower

4) **I will continue to strongly recruit a prospect if I hear from or interact with their parents/guardians more frequently than I do with the prospect.**
Mean Response: 4.2
Median Response: 4
Most Common Response: 5*
Scholarship level mean response: 4.1
Non-scholarship level mean response: 4.3
Control Group mean: 3.34 (note, one coach corresponded with an 8 or higher)
Response clustering (if applicable): 80% of total responses were a 5 or lower
*10% of coaches responded with an 8 or higher

5) **I refer to an athlete's stats at the High School/Club level when making recruiting decisions.**
Mean Response: 4.5
Median Response: 5
Most Common Response: 5
Scholarship level mean response: 4.8
Non-scholarship level mean response: 4.2
Control Group mean: 4.6
Response clustering (if applicable): n/a

Section 2: Evaluations and the Filtering Process
(1 = Completely Disagree, 10 = Completely Agree)

1) **The position the recruit plays in high school is the position they will play on my team throughout their college career.**
   Mean Response: 3.1
   Median Response: 3
   Most Common Response: 1
   Scholarship level mean response: 4.1
   Non-scholarship level mean response: 2.
   Control Group mean: 2.8
   Response clustering (if applicable): 82% of total responses were a 5 or lower

2) **A prospect I am seriously recruiting is able to accurately speak to their own strengths and limitations pertaining to their sport performance.**
   Mean Response: 7
   Median Response: 7
   Most Common Response: 8
   Scholarship level mean response: 6.9
   Non-scholarship level mean response: 7.2
   Control Group mean: 6.5
   Response clustering (if applicable): 80% of total responses were a 6 or higher

3) **The average high school-aged recruit understands the scope and magnitude of being a college athlete.**
   Mean Response: 3.5
   Median Response: 3

Most Common Response: 2.5
Scholarship level mean response: 3.4
Non-scholarship level mean response: 3.5
Control Group mean: 2.7
Response clustering (if applicable): 82% of total responses were a 5 or lower

4) **During initial conversations with a recruit, I evaluate them based on their level of engagement with me.**
Mean Response: 6.9
Median Response: 7
Most Common Response: 6
Scholarship level mean response: 7.5
Non-scholarship level mean response: 6.5
Control Group mean: 5.9
Response clustering (if applicable): 82% of total responses were a 6 or higher

5) **I evaluate recruits based on the quality of their questions in conversations with me.**
Mean Response: 6.2
Median Response: 7
Most Common Response: 7
Scholarship level mean response: 6.4
Non-scholarship level mean response: 6
Control Group mean: 5
Response clustering (if applicable): n/a

6) **What is the lowest performance level x/10 you would take on your team for someone with a 10/10 attitude who was unconditionally trustworthy?**
Mean Response: 5

Median Response: 5
Most Common Response: 5
Scholarship level mean response: 5.4
Non-scholarship level mean response: 4.5
Control Group mean: 4.5
Response clustering (if applicable): 75% of responses fell between a 4 and a 6

7) **What is the lowest attitude level x/10 you would take on your team for someone that was a 10/10 performance?**

Mean Response: 5.7
Median Response: 5
Most Common Response: 5
Scholarship level mean response: 6.2
Non-scholarship level mean response: 5.1
Control Group mean: 5.8
Response clustering (if applicable): 74% of responses fell between a 5 and an 8

Section 3: Visits and "Fit" Finding
(1 = Completely Disagree, 10 = Completely Agree)

1) **A positive and engaging unofficial/official visit can move a recruit from a "maybe" up to a "yes."**
   Mean Response: 8.5
   Median Response: 9
   Most Common Response: 10
   Scholarship level mean response: 8.5
   Non-scholarship level mean response: 8.4
   Control Group mean: 9.3
   Response clustering (if applicable): 78% of total responses were an 8 or higher

2) **A negative and disengaged unofficial/official visit can move a recruit from a "yes" to a "maybe" or a "no."**
   Mean Response: 8.6
   Median Response: 9
   Most Common Response: 10
   Scholarship level mean response: 8.9
   Non-scholarship level mean response: 8.3
   Control Group mean: 9.3
   Response clustering (if applicable): 82% of total responses were an 8 or higher

3) **I solicit feedback from current players about a recruit at the end of a recruit's campus visit.**
   Mean Response: 9.4
   Median Response: 10
   Most Common Response: 10

Scholarship level mean response: 9.7
Non-scholarship level mean response: 9.1
Control Group mean: 9.1
Response clustering (if applicable): 88% of total responses were a 9 or higher

4) **When circumstances permit, our staff ideally offers roster spots to recruits in person.**
Mean Response: 7.8
Median Response: 9
Most Common Response: 10
Scholarship level mean response: 7.7
Non-scholarship level mean response: 7.9
Control Group mean: 8.6
Response clustering (if applicable): n/a

5) **When we offer a roster spot to a recruit, we expect a decision immediately.**
Mean Response: 2
Median Response: 1
Most Common Response: 1
Scholarship level mean response: 2.3
Non-scholarship level mean response: 1.8
Control Group mean: 1.3
Response clustering (if applicable): 72% of total responses were a 2 or lower

ANECDOTAL NOTES

*In response to the open-ended questions,
the below themes emerged:*

In the time since you started coaching, have you noticed any significant changes to recruiting that you think are worth discussing with high school students?

a) There is a higher level of social media impression and influence on the process.
b) Recruits' preferred methods of communication have changed. They're particularly less interested in verbal communication (i.e. on the phone or in person).
c) AAU programs/events are over-saturating the recruiting space. Athletes are also playing too many games and not spending enough time refining their skills.
d) There is less of an emphasis on relationship building during the process.
e) Parents want to be involved in the process earlier (especially at the non-scholarship level, due to financial implications).
f) A single-sport focus has developed among many high school-aged athletes.

g) There is a growing trend of college coaches who leverage the transfer portal earlier than they previously would have and engage with high school-aged prospects later than they previously would have (i.e. starting to recruit a prospect in the summer of their junior year instead of their sophomore year, etc).

What is your biggest recruiting "red flag?"

a) Parents that demonstrate an excessive level of involvement in multiplate facets of their child's process (examples included: badmouthing opponents/coaches/refs, not allowing children to fail, inflated views of their child's attitude or ability, children looking to parents before looking to coaches for instruction).

b) A prospect who displayed poor attitude/body language in-game and on the sidelines would turn off a coach evaluating them.

c) A prospect engages in disrespectful and/or offensive behavior either in person or on social media.

d) The prospect in question displays a poor work ethic or poor response to mistakes.

e) There is a pronounced lack of engagement from the prospect to the coaching staff recruiting them (unreturned calls/texts, disinterest on campus visits etc.).

f) A recruit has played on multiple High School and/or Club Teams without explanation. Coaches often interpret this as a sign that the prospect cannot handle being held accountable by a coach.

NAIL THE RECRUITING PROCESS

How do you handle over involved parents during the process?

a) Nearly half of all respondents articulated a strategy where they attempt to re-direct communication directly to the prospect. If that didn't work, they would attempt to have an honest conversation with the parent about their need to take a step back.
b) Staffs will schedule intentional time with the prospect and staff on visits without parents present.
c) Coaches will establish clear boundaries with parents during the recruiting process and make sure parents know they can always talk about their child's safety with a coach, but that other conversations will be limited once the recruit matriculates.
d) More than 25% of respondents indicated that they would stop recruiting a prospect after multiple failed attempts at re-directing and setting expectations with parents.

Is there anything else you think would be important for a recruit to know?

a) The more engaged you are in the process, the better the results will be.
b) Ask yourself hard questions to confirm your top school is an actual fit.
c) Be able to identify the difference between good people and good stuff.
d) Do not enter the recruiting process banking on the transfer portal later in your journey.
e) Know your "red flags" and take extra visits to ensure you've discovered all of them.

f) Do your homework in advance of a call or visit with a coach.
g) Your recruiting process isn't over once you've arrived on campus for the start of your first year.
h) Do not let external factors and comparison distract or sadden you.

MY FINAL PLEA

Thank you so much for reading my book!

I'm a coach, which means I'm powered
by assessment and reflection.
Your feedback REALLY matters to me.

I need your help to make future versions of
this book and my next projects better.

Please take a few minutes and leave a helpful review:
NailTheRecruitingProcess.com/review

Thanks again, and best of luck in your recruiting journey!

-Jared

www.ingramcontent.com/pod-product-compliance
Lightning Source LLC
Chambersburg PA
CBHW020935090426
42736CB00010B/1151